WHAT '80s

POP CULTURE
TEACHES US ABOUT
TODAY'S WORKPLACE

10 MORE ICONIC MOVIES,
EVEN MORE TOTALLY AWESOME
BUSINESS LESSONS

PRAISE FOR *WHAT '80s POP CULTURE TEACHES US ABOUT TODAY'S WORKPLACE,* BOOK #2

"Finally! Author Chris Clews makes you feel better about blowing half your life re-watching classic eighties flicks."

Kevin Barnett

Screenwriter and Producer, *Hall Pass, The Heartbreak Kid,* and Other Well-Known Projects

"Chris Clews mines our shared cultural signposts, including the movies we love, for insights that stick and that can make a difference in our work and our lives. Add this book to your collection!"

Ed Saxon

Academy Award Winning Producer, Storyteller, and Speaker

"Who knew that the popular culture of our youth would become a map to our professional success?"

Joe Cox
Creator of The Pop-Marketer

"Chris not only has corporate marketing experience and an understanding of what is needed in today's working world, but he has also has done something no one else has done ... by artfully crafting simple lessons revolving around his passion of the '80s that will open up your mind and your heart ... I am thrilled to be part of Chris's crusade to make the workplace triumphant. His perspectives and insights bring valuable lessons to the office and are effective, fun and easy to remember."

Diane Franklin
Iconic '80s actress from *The Last American Virgin, Better Off Dead* and *Bill and Ted's Excellent Adventure*

"I'm a huge fan of numerous leadership books, yet never would have thought '80s movies could teach me something about our workplaces and organization. Chris Clews has found a new way to interpret these iconic films."

Dan Leonard
President, Margaritaville Hospitality Group

"Chris Clews has found a way to tap into nostalgia for my youth (oh yes, the '80s were my years) as well as tantalize my passion to continually develop myself as a leader. This book captivated me from the first quote, making me ponder the lessons while frequently laughing out loud. As a leadership author, speaker and trainer, I challenge my audiences to become lifelong students, always seeking out new ideas. Chris takes the core messages from iconic films and boils them down to mantras we can (and should!) strive to live by as leaders. The fresh approach to this book provides a unique vehicle in which to navigate an ongoing leadership journey, encouraging that lifelong student to view something as simple as a movie with an eye for the lessons buried within.

Michael Sherlock

Transformational Leader, Shock Your Potential Podcast Host, Speaker, and Author of *Tell Me More: How to Ask the Right Questions and Get the Most Out of Your Employees* and *Sales Mixology: Why the Most Potent Sales and Customer Experiences Follow a Recipe for Success*

"The way that Chris intertwines lessons from our favorite childhood movies into our current workplace and businesses is inspiring. He is a master of all things '80s and has a knack for bridging the gap between what we learned as children and how to apply it as adults!"

Kyle Autrey and Justin DiSandro

The Back in Time Podcast

"Chris has found a way to extract business wisdom out of the '80s movies and songs many of us hold so dear. A truly enjoyable and nostalgic read with golden nuggets of business advice throughout."

Karen Jones

Executive Vice President and Chief Marketing Officer, Ryder

"We are thrilled to be partnering with Chris again to help animals in crisis across the world. Chris embodies the workplace lessons in his book and has found a really unique way to interpret '80s movies, even lending compassion to that unruly gopher in *Caddyshack*."

Meredith Ayan
Executive Director, SPCA International

"Chris has a keen insight and ability to distill business lessons that resonate universally from the fun, unique and campy movies of the 1980s. Who could have guessed the entertainment we enjoyed in the '80s would become a platform for business lessons we experience today!"

Jim Garfield
Sports Marketing Executive and Professional Adventure Athlete

WHAT '80s

POP CULTURE TEACHES US ABOUT TODAY'S WORKPLACE

10 MORE ICONIC MOVIES, EVEN MORE TOTALLY AWESOME BUSINESS LESSONS

Book #2

CHRIS CLEWS

FOREWORD BY DIANE FRANKLIN, ACTRESS FROM
THE LAST AMERICAN VIRGIN, BETTER OFF DEAD
AND *BILL AND TED'S EXCELLENT ADVENTURE*

SILVER TREE
PUBLISHING

"You had to be big shots, didn't you? You had to show off. When are you gonna learn that people will like you for who you are, not for what you can give them?"

Lisa, *Weird Science*

DEDICATION

This book series is dedicated many special people.

To my best friend, Dex, who passed in 2008 and had the greatest smile the world has ever known.

To John Hughes, who shaped and formed my teenage years and is the reason I will always wax nostalgic for the '80s.

Chris and Dex, Circa 1988

To Ferris Bueller, for always reminding me to embrace every day.

Those '80s boardwalk arcades that took all my quarters during my summer quest to solve *Dragon's Lair* but taught me to never give up.

To my amazing family and incredible friends for their unwavering support.

To all the people who work or volunteer with animal rescues around the world.

To everyone who bought my first book and everyone reading this for investing in an unknown author and giving me the ability to chase my dream.

And to everyone out there who dreams big. Dream bigger. And then make it your reality.

TABLE OF CONTENTS

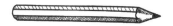

"I'm going to give you a little advice. There's a force in the universe that makes things happen. And all you have to do is get in touch with it, stop thinking, let things happen, and be the ball."

Ty Webb, *Caddyshack*

FOREWORD

by Diane Franklin

Greetings, dudes and babes! My name is Diane Franklin, and I was an '80s actress. You might remember me as the dream girl, Karen, in the iconic teen film *The Last American Virgin*. Or as the French exchange student, Monique Junot, from the classic comedy *Better Off Dead*. Or perhaps as the Medieval babe, Princess Joanna, from the original *Bill & Ted's Excellent Adventure*!

I am sooo excited to introduce Chris Clews's second book in his awesome series, *What '80s Pop Culture Teaches Us About Today's Workplace*. It is *most* inspired because Chris not only has corporate marketing experience and an understanding of what is needed in today's working world, but he has also done something no one else has done ... by artfully crafting simple lessons — revolving around his passion of the '80s — that will open up your mind and your heart.

When I started acting, I had no idea how my acting roles would affect other people's lives so deeply, and yet they did, and they still do. I even met someone once who told me he "made sure not to get his girlfriend pregnant" after seeing me in a film! Ha! *Well, glad I could help.* My film roles have shown characters with self-motivation, resilience, optimism, fearlessness and love. The same thing can apply to you. You affect other people every day at your job. You have such an impact on the world. Your actions can make the difference.

In the workplace, this way of thinking is golden! Rather than look for problems, complain or blame, why not compliment, praise, or fix the problem yourself? If someone needs motivation, say what Monique would say ... *"You can do it!"* Positive comments make people feel good, inspire them to want to work *with* you, and make the workplace a *most excellent* place!

I am thrilled to be part of Chris's crusade to make the workplace triumphant. His perspectives and insights bring valuable lessons to the office and are effective, fun and easy to remember. So, enjoy this super-fun ride back to the '80s. And who knows? You just might learn some *very* valuable business lessons (while recalling some '80s "language lessons" along the way).

xo,
Diane Franklin

CHAPTER 1

THE OUTSIDERS

"Stay Gold, Ponyboy. Stay Gold."

Johnny, *The Outsiders*

As I sit down to write this second book, I have the 1983 movie, *The Outsiders*, on mute in the background and the '80s channel playing on SiriusXM radio. I'm in my element and feeling nostalgic for the time when I would lay in my front yard on a summer night looking up at the stars and wondering who I might become. My whole life in front of me and as Tom Petty said in his 1989 hit "Runnin' Down a Dream," "Felt so good like anything was possible." It is in that moment where there is an opportunity to **Create You,** and yet so many of us put that off for way too many years. We settle, and then we settle into a life, career, and the daily grind. In fact, it took a Greaser in *The Outsiders* named Johnny Cade to remind me that we still have plenty of time "to make yourself be what you want."

And when you envision a group of kids called The Greasers, the picture you paint in your head likely doesn't include a literary work, "Nothing Gold Can Stay" from the poet, Robert Frost. It's also likely that it doesn't evoke words of wisdom that can be applied to the business world in the area of ethics, but two Greasers, in particular, will teach us a lot about **never losing sight of your moral and ethical compass.** How we need to "stay gold" no matter how intense the situation within our business has become and remember that our business and our human legacy will be built on how we handle the worst of times rather than the best.

As we continue to think about leadership, we often hear and see that those who reach a certain level of success can forget where they came from. This chapter concludes with a short bonus lesson on leadership that comes from an impossible love story between Ponyboy from the "wrong" side of the tracks and Cherry Valance from the "right" side of the tracks.

DIGRESSION ALERT: Ugh, now I have the 1987 song "Right on Track" from the one-hit wonders, *The Breakfast Club*, in my head.

Ponyboy and Cherry live in very different worlds, but as Ponyboy sits on his porch, he thinks about how, regardless of their background and station in life, they also live under the same sunset. **Great leaders recognize that we all see the same sunset** and approach all their employees with that equality in mind.

So before we expand on the lessons that *The Outsiders* taught us for the workplace, let's hop in the DeLorean and take a quick look back at 1983:

In March of that year, I was in the throes of a middle school career that saw fashion faux pas like a 4-inch-long rat-tail, parachute pants, a sweet red Members Only jacket and a Panama Jack hat complete with awkward sun shading flaps in the back. So weird. The '80s had a ton of awesome, but fashion was not amongst its better qualities.

> ***The '80s had a ton of awesome, but fashion was not amongst its better qualities.***

The music charts were doing what the music charts did in the '80s — and of course, what made them eclectic and amazing — providing us with a cacophony of sounds that would span the musical whimsies of even the most varied of groups. Groups like say, "a brain, athlete, basket case, princess and a criminal" (i.e., The Breakfast Club). Michael Jackson held the top spot with "Billie Jean" while Bob Seger and The Silver Bullet Band were holding down the #2 spot with "Shame on the Moon." Thomas Dolby was "blinding us with science" while we learned about "passing the dutchie" via Musical Youth. Saga was "On the Loose," and Prince was chasing down a "Little Red Corvette." If you really want an example of how varied popular music was in the '80s, look no further than two of the acts that dropped out of the Top 40 the same week — Mr. Sweet Caroline himself, Neil Diamond, and he of the "Goody Two Shoes," Adam Ant. Gotta love musical diversity.

In television, we said goodbye to *M*A*S*H,* viewing the final episode along with 106 million[1] of our closest friends, and *Little House on the Prairie,* which I can honestly say I've never seen (and probably never will). One of my favorites, *The Greatest American Hero,* "walked on air" for the last time. I mean just to digress for a moment — that is one great theme song — "Believe it or not, I'm walking on air. I never thought I could feel so free ..." And, yes, you can thank me for that being stuck in your head for the next day or two.

 FUN FACT: In the *Seinfeld* episode "The Susie," George Constanza uses a personalized version of The Greatest American Hero theme song, "Believe It or Not," for his answering machine message. Answering machines ... wow, I kind of miss the anticipation of what or who might be behind the red blinking light when I got home.

Okay, so back to the small screen. From those that ended to those that began, we were introduced to the original *America's Got Talent* in the form of *Star Search,* the mini-series *The Thorn Birds* (which I'm convinced my mom watched over 100 times and would again if it was on Netflix today) and Hannibal, Murdock, Face and B.A. in *The A-Team.* Alright, so actually *The A-Team* premiered in January of '83, but Mr. T is

---

1   https://www.washingtonpost.com/news/morning-mix/
wp/2018/02/28/106-million-people-watched-mash-finale-35-years-ago-
no-scripted-show-has-come-close-since/

one of my all-time favorites so anytime I can find a way to include him, I absolutely will.

The box office was dominated by a cross-dressing actor, a bio-pic about one of the most peaceful humans to inhabit the Earth, two foul-mouthed and hilarious detectives and the most peaceful *alien* to inhabit the Earth ... for a short time anyway. *Tootsie, Gandhi, 48 Hours* and *E.T.* were all raking in plenty of $2.00 movie tickets. Yes, Virginia, movie tickets in 1983 were two bucks, which I guess is why the paperboy in *Better Off Dead* was so adamant about collecting his "Two dollars ... cash" (which has a lesson that will be revealed in Chapter 7 — don't peek!).

On March 25th, *The Outsiders* premiered in theatres across the nation with a cast that would never be heard from again in Hollywood. (Okay, yes, I was absolutely sitting on my very own "throne of lies" as I typed those words.) Directed by Francis Ford Coppola, the film version of the classic novel written by S.E. Hinton was brought to life by C. Thomas Howell, Matt Dillon, Ralph Macchio, Patrick Swayze (man I miss that guy), Rob Lowe, Emilio Estevez, Tom Cruise and Diane Lane.

Likely set in Tulsa, Oklahoma, *The Outsiders* tells the story of two gangs — The Greasers and the Socs — with the focus on the former. Ponyboy Curtis, Sodapop, Darrel (Darry), Johnny Cade, Dallas Winston (Dally), Two-Bit and Steve Randle are the main Greasers who are blue-collar and from the wrong side of the tracks while the Socs are comprised of kids from the wealthy section of town. Early in the film, a fight ensues over love and romance — with Johnny and Ponyboy getting jumped by five

Socs, resulting in the stabbing death of the main Soc instigator, Bob, at the hands of Johnny Cade.

Even though self-defense could probably be argued, the two boys flee and hide out in a church outside of town while the rest of the Greasers provide support. After one of the girls — Cherry — agrees to testify in support of Johnny, they decide to come back (but not before they grab a bite to eat). On their way back to the church to grab their things, they see that it's on fire with children trapped inside. They decide to make an attempt to save the children — which they do — but in the process, Johnny is severely injured and close to death.

Before he dies in the hospital, he tells Ponyboy to "stay gold," which is from a Robert Frost poem, "Nothing Gold Can Stay." Another Frost poem, "The Road Less Taken" is also invoked in one of my favorite movies of all time, *Dead Poets Society,* but I digress — as I often do. A series of unfortunate events unfold from Johnny's death, but eventually, Ponyboy is able to tell his tragic story of courage and bravery.

Before he dies in the hospital, he tells Ponyboy to "stay gold."

There's so much more tell about S.E. Hinton's literary master-piece that we could dissect in a book of its own. And any movie that has the great Patrick Swayze should have its own spot in the Library of Congress with an induction into The National Film Registry, so if anyone reading this can make that happen, please let me know.

So what did the brat pack gang of Greasers from *The Outsiders* teach us about today's workplace?

 Never lose sight of your moral and ethical compass.

As we learned above, when Johnny says, "Stay gold, Ponyboy, stay gold," he is in the hospital and close to death after saving the lives of children in a burning church. The entire group of Greasers have had incredibly difficult lives growing up on the wrong side of the tracks and being vilified for anything bad that happens in town. Johnny Cade comes from a background of abuse at home but is the least violent of the Greasers and often serves as kind of a moral compass for the gang even when he makes the decision to stab Bob since he is protecting Ponyboy. Despite his heart being in the right place, he is an incredibly vulnerable character which is not a good trait to have in his world and is the cause of several incidents where he is on the wrong end of a violent attack.

~~~~~~

 DIGRESSION ALERT: It's interesting that Ralph Macchio played two of the more vulnerable characters in '80s films — Johnny Cade and the receiver of philosophical thought like "wax on, wax off," Daniel LaRusso in *The Karate Kid* (the original and only — no more '80s remakes please. You'll hear that from me a lot. It's my life mission). And if you took more than a glance at the table of contents, you may have seen that we

will have a conversation later in the book about all things wise from the immortal Mr. Miyagi.

Back to the lesson. So, with everything that Johnny has been through and the incredibly difficult, violent life he was born into and with no real opportunity to do better, he still chooses to run into a burning church in an attempt to save the children trapped inside. In his dying breaths, he implores Ponyboy to "stay gold" — to continue to be good no matter the situation and always look for the right thing to do in any circumstance ... regardless of how hard it may be.

Herein lies our lesson. This is for everyone in life and in business but most importantly for those in leadership or management positions and for those who are building or who have built their own business. Just like life, our workplace has ups and downs. And just like in life, when things are going well, our character is rarely tested. You are hitting your numbers; the company is growing, cash on hand is up, every account you chase you land and well, things couldn't be going better. When everything is going your way; it's easy to "stay gold."

Just like life, our workplace has ups and downs. And just like in life, when things are going well, our character is rarely tested.

But you know it's coming at some point — you'll miss your numbers; you won't land the big account, or even worse you'll lose your biggest one. Cash is down, and borrowing is up. Your team or staff is shrinking, and project deadlines are missed. They are feeling the stress, and so are you. Things are spiraling out of control, and the boulders at the bottom of the proverbial hill get bigger and bigger. Everything just seems impossible. This is when the decisions that you make will have the largest impact on your business and more importantly, the people that depend on you and your leadership in the workplace. It's when your workplace morale and ethical compasses will be tested. It's when it is the most important time to "stay gold," and for some, it will also be the most difficult time to do the right thing.

The stress of a business or department that is failing — even if for just a short time — is more than some leaders can handle and they lash out at their teams or employees for no reason other than their inability to cope. They say and write things that begin to create a difficult and even hostile environment for everyone, many of who are not in the least bit responsible for the current situation. They play the blame game with their 10 fingers and 10 toes all pointing outward toward someone else who is usually at a lower level. Pretty sure we've all experienced this person. And if most of your leadership is what is referred to as "jellyfish" or to use an '80s term "dweebs," then be prepared for the proverbial circular firing squad. The political world thrives on this idea of no one taking responsibility. But again, I digress.

A minority will ultimately resort to actions that are unethical at best and sometimes criminal as they seek the easy and self-ishly painless way out until, of course, either karma catches up with them (which is absolutely real — just ask the Alpha Betas in *Revenge of the Nerds*) or prison (à la Gordon Gecko) comes a-knockin.'

True leaders will keep their ethical and moral compasses intact, even sacrificing themselves to ensure that their team, business and employees are protected from whatever is ailing the workplace. They don't do this because there is something in it for them. No. They do it because it is the right and noble thing to do, and it is what separates those that lead from those who rule. These are the times that your legacy is built and these are the times to invoke your inner Ponyboy Curtis and "stay gold."

> **These are the times that your legacy is built**
> **and these are the times to invoke your**
> **inner Ponyboy Curtis and "stay gold."**

Create You

Once again, Johnny Cade is responsible for one of our lessons from *The Outsiders*. Earlier in the film, Johnny and Ponyboy share a copy of the book *Gone with the Wind* but do not finish it before Johnny passes away. He leaves Ponyboy the book, and when he finally opens it, a note falls out that Johnny left for him. The note says that he is okay with sacrificing his life for the children as they will probably amount to more than he ever would and more importantly it tells Ponyboy that he has much more to offer than being a Greaser.

The note is short, but each word has meaning, and the moment is both heartbreaking and uplifting. Even if you haven't seen the movie — which in the words of Ozzy Osbourne circa 1980 is just "Crazy Train" — do yourself a favor and Google it. It doesn't need the context to move you.

One of the lines toward the end of the note reads, *"You still have a lot of time to make yourself be what you want."* This one really resonates with me. At the time of this writing (wow, that sounds so captain-of-a-ship-in-1610 filling in his diary), I am 48 years young and within the last 12 months I have written a book, working on the second in the series which happens to be this one, spoken at conferences on the topic of '80s movies and workplace lessons, been a guest on a number of podcasts and am moving closer to leaving the corporate world forever to spend the rest of my life writing and speaking. It took me 48 years of life and 23 years in my career to find that moment of inspiration to create me and be what I want.

Many of us daydream at our jobs. It's okay, you can admit it. No one from work is around. And unlike the daydreams of our youth, these are usually more about where we would like to be in our career or more likely what career we would like to have. But then we come back to the reality of conference calls, meetings, desks piled with work and the ever-present Buzzword Bob whose presence graces every meeting with words and phrases like "synergy," "let's put a pin in it," "move the needle" and limited bandwidth."

Coming back to reality is a good thing. I mean, our jobs and careers are important to all of us and being able to focus is a major component of success. But daydreaming doesn't have to be just a dream, and it most certainly doesn't have an age limit. If you find yourself at work and at home consistently thinking about a passion project that continues to find a little space in your head whether its 1pm or 1am, then it's time to make that dream a reality. Don't be afraid to walk out on that plank and take your leap of faith. It doesn't matter if you're in your first job or are a seasoned executive and leader, as Johnny Cade said, *"You still have a lot of time to make yourself be what you want."* Create you. I did it, and so can you.

> **It doesn't matter if you're in your first job or are a seasoned executive and leader, as Johnny Cade said, "You still have a lot of time to make yourself be what you want."**

Great leaders recognize that we all see the same sunset.

This is a short bonus lesson that I wanted to throw in because (a) it's severely needed in leadership and (b) it revolves around one of my favorite lines in the movie.

Throughout the movie, Ponyboy, a Greaser, and Cherry Valance, a Soc girlfriend, from the "right" neighborhood, clearly have a connection. Because she dated a Soc and because of their class differences, it's difficult for them to have more than a cursory relationship throughout most of the story, but she realizes Ponyboy is different and at one point says to him, "You read a lot don't you, Ponyboy. I can just tell. I bet you watch sunsets, too."

When he reflects on this short but poignant conversation, Ponyboy says to himself:

> *"It seemed funny to me that the sunset she saw from her patio and the one I saw from the back steps was the same one. Maybe the two different worlds we lived in weren't so different. We saw the same sunset."*

And herein lies our lesson for leaders. As you advance in your career or build your own business, you will begin leading teams that are larger in size, and they will be compromised of a wonderfully diverse set of people from all walks of life. These teams that you lead could include other executives, middle management, entry-level positions and interns. And if you build your own business, your leadership style will even be felt by the people you don't always see. The people who clean the office at night, so everyone has a respectable and comfortable place to work. The people who provide the security to keep everyone safe. The people who work in the kitchen and provide the meals and meeting food that so many take for granted. The people who work in the mailroom delivering the documents that can sometimes make or break a quarter or a year.

These are the people who are the lifeblood of a company and great leaders recognize that all of us, regardless of our station in life, compensation package or title will go home tonight and *"See the same sunset."* Remember, as you advance in your career or grow your business to treat everyone with respect and appreciation regardless of where they may view the sunset. That's what truly great leaders do, and we need more of them.

> ***Remember, as you advance in your career or grow your business to treat everyone with respect and appreciation regardless of where they may view the sunset.***

CHAPTER 2

THE PRINCESS BRIDE

"My name is Inigo Montoya. You killed my Father. Prepare to die."

Inigo Montoya, *The Princess Bride*

Two of the things that make a movie great for me are (a) an ensemble cast of unforgettable characters and (b) dialogue so quotable that decades later it is ingrained in the fabric of our language. *The Princess Bride* easily checks both of these boxes. In the ensemble corner, we had Cary Elwes, Robin Wright Penn, Billy Crystal, Andre the Giant, Carol Kane, Peter Falk, Fred Savage, Christopher Guest, Wallace Shawn, Chris Sarandon and of course Mandy Patinkin as the bent-on revenge, lovable and mediocre swashbuckler, Inigo Montoya.

If the movie had been set in 1980 rather than what looks like the Middle Ages, Inigo would have made a fantastic marketer.

His message to everyone he meets: "Hello. My name is Inigo Montoya. You killed my father. Prepare to die" — is crystal clear and breakthrough-the-clutter bold, which makes it marketing gold. The rhyming there was unintentional, although that line might have fit nicely into some late '80s hip hop — say maybe my favorite by far, L.L. Cool J and his 1987 hit song, "I'm Bad," which had lyrics like, "I'm the best takin' out all rookies so forget Oreos eat Cool J cookies." Just awesome. But back to Inigo and his messaging prowess.

> *If the movie had been set in 1980 rather than what looks like the Middle Ages, Inigo would have made a fantastic marketer.*

Just like Inigo, successful brands and marketers don't hide their intentions from their target audience. They are clear. They are honest. They are bold.

Being quotable is also a quality of a great movie — at least in my eyes — and *The Princess Bride* might just be in the top 10 of this category. Besides Inigo's bold message, the volume of quotable quotes could keep an extended family busy enough at a Thanksgiving dinner to avoid political discussions and that one crazy uncle from serenading the group with his very bad karaoke version of "We Built This City" by Jefferson Starship.

> *Being quotable is also a quality of a great movie — at least in my eyes — and* **The Princess Bride** *might just be in the top 10 of this category.*

Quotes like "Inconceivable," "Anybody want a peanut?" "Please consider me as an alternative to suicide," "You keep using that word. I do not think it means what you think it means," "You're trying to kidnap what I've rightfully stolen," "Goodnight, Westley. Good work. Sleep well. I'll most likely kill you in the morning," and "As you wish." Hopefully, you've never uttered those last three words at work when you've been asked to do something, but you've likely said "yes" and you've probably said it way too much. Just as important as accepting new tasks and projects at work, so is also **learning to say no** — which our determined farm boy and part-time pirate, Westley, will teach us in this chapter.

So, before we really learn what *The Princess Bride* taught us about the workplace, let's fire up our time-traveling phone booth and take an excellent adventure à la *Bill and Ted*, back to the fall of 1987.

It was October, and I was in my final year of high school hurtling toward a life without forced geometry, physics and woodshop all of which I'm convinced were designed to dismantle any confidence I had in myself. How bad was it? Well, I only passed geometry because a very good friend let me look over her shoulder during tests. Not for free, of course. Nope. I had to figure out a way to buy the Bartles and Jaymes "thank you for your support" berry wine coolers for the house parties we attended. Physics? Well, back then, to pass the class, you had to build a bridge out of what I recall were toothpicks, popsicle sticks and Elmer's Glue. Said bridge was entered in a stress test where it had to hold the equivalent of 10 to 38 lbs. Well, mine broke at five lbs., so yeah, I'm not a bridge builder or anywhere close to an engineer. Yes, you are still completely safe with the infrastructure in your area. Last but not least, woodshop. You could say that in a nod to the great 1984 *SNL*

(*Saturday Night Live*) synchronized swimming skit with Martin Short where he says, "I'm not that strong of a swimmer," — well, "I'm not that strong of a carpenter." Our project was making a napkin holder with an animal shape (I still don't know why), and I decided on a whale. The final result was a napkin holder that didn't have enough space between the whale and posts to hold more than two napkins. Two. If you are wondering, that does not garner a passing grade. And bless my mom as she still displays it proudly on the kitchen table. Or maybe it's just her subtle way of poking me every time I come home. Yeah, that's a real possibility.

Now, as a reminder, it is October of 1987, and the Top 40 is just as interesting as ever. Musical acts with the word "boys" in them were very popular as evidenced by The Pet Shop Boys with "It's a Sin," "Wipeout" by the Fat Boys and the Beach Boys gracing the charts. In an ode to the eclectic nature of popular '80s music, The Grateful Dead came out with "Touch of Grey," Levert with "Casanova" and Whitesnake held the #1 spot with "Here I Go Again."

In television, several series debuted that unbeknownst to them were preparing for long successful runs and mentions in popular culture for years to come. *Alf*, the lovable but crass alien life form (ALF — get it?), *Thirtysomething* (which I can't believe is actually a decade behind me although my crow's feet make it easier to believe) and *Star Trek: The Next Generation*, (which set the bar for overacting and remains a favorite mention by the crew in *Big Bang Theory)*. Earlier in the year, we said a tearful goodbye to *Gimme a Break* and the endearing Nell Carter while we prepared to send *The Jetsons* permanently into the future.

FUN FACT: *The Jetsons* **was set in the year 2062, and George Jetson had a 3-hour, 3-day work-week, so maybe they actually predicted the existence of Tim Ferris and his 4-Hour Workweek.**

We were also about a month away from *The Transformers* ending its television run and going on temporary hiatus until Michael Bay decided to bring his "let's blow stuff up in the coolest way ever" movie-making style to the series.

At the box office, *Fatal Attraction* taught married couples that affairs are never a good idea, especially if you have a pet rabbit and a way to boil water. Richard Dreyfuss dancing to Gloria Estefan and the Miami Sound Machine's "Rhythm Is Gonna Get You" and Emilio Estevez's awkward mustache made us laugh out loud in *Stakeout. Hello Mary Lou: Prom Night 2,* was the latest '80s slasher film entry. I never saw it, but you can be sure that someone fell while running away from a killer that was walking and then died a horrible death in a cabin while making love after their car didn't start.

The week of October 5th, 1987, *The Princess Bride* was released nationwide. For '80s movie historians — man, I wish they had '80s movie history as a major when I was in college — its true release date was September 25th, but that was in nine theaters only. Directed by Rob Reiner, it follows a farmhand named Westley and his band of eccentric, lovable and merry people.

FUN FACT: I met Andre the Giant when I was in elementary school, and my dad was directing a Pro Wrestling show. Still have the autograph but can't find the picture and I look every time I go back home. I remember how insanely huge he was and how, when he put his hand on my head, it covered my face as well. I also remember how nice, kind and down to earth he was.

The story of *The Princess Bride* is being read to a sick boy — played by Fred Savage of *Wonder Years* fame — by his grandfather played by Peter Falk. The essentials are as follows: A young woman named Buttercup and her farmhand Westley fall in love. During his quest to find riches he disappears and is presumed dead from an encounter with the Dread Pirate Roberts.

Years later, she is set to marry Prince Humperdinck, who is as charming as his name and not at all who she desires. She is kidnapped before the ceremony by three bandits, including one of the characters that will teach us a very valuable lesson — Inigo Montoya. Throughout the movie, Prince Humperdinck and Westley, who is referred to as the Man in Black, chase the bandits with the goal of saving Buttercup.

During the 98 minutes, the main cast run into a number of interesting characters including a healer/magician, Miracle Max and his wife, played brilliantly as usual by Billy Crystal and Carol Kane, Vizzini made famous by Wallace Shawn and one word "inconceivable" and my favorite Andre the Giant as Fezzik who is, well, a giant. It's an incredible cast of characters that deliver a multitude of memorable scenes that made *The Princess Bride* a cult classic that is still entertaining new generations 30-plus years later. And, of course, as a fairytale is apt to do, it does have a happy ending but not before we get this classic exchange:

> **Inigo**: "Fezzik, are there rocks ahead?"
>
> **Fezzik**: "If there are, you'll be dead."
>
> **Vizzini**: "No more rhymes, I mean it!"
>
> **Fezzik**: "Anybody want a peanut?"

Google it. It's amazing.

So, what did our band of fairytale characters from *The Princess Bride* teach us about today's workplace:

 Don't hide your intentions from your target audience. Be clear. Be honest. Be bold.

Throughout the movie, three lines are repeated on a number of occasions with the first two being "As you wish" and "Inconceivable." But it is the third one that teaches us a valuable lesson about the workplace.

When we first meet Inigo Montoya, he is with his two companions — Fezzik (the Giant) and Vizzini (the Sicilian) — who have kidnapped Buttercup. As they race for their destination across the water, they are chased by the Man in Black. He eventually catches up to them at the Cliffs of Insanity, and when Inigo and the Man in Black finally meet with swords drawn, Inigo asks him if he has "six fingers on his hand" which prompts the story of why he would start a conversation with a question like that. He says that his father was killed by a man with six fingers when he was a boy, and it is here that we learn Inigo's mission in life — revenge. He makes this clear when he says that the next time he sees the six-fingered man, he will say to him: *"Hello. My name is Inigo Montoya. You killed my father. Prepare to die."*

As the movie progresses, Inigo eventually finds the six-fingered man and tells him five times in a matter of minutes, *"Hello. My name is Inigo Montoya. You killed my father. Prepare to die."* Marketing people like myself would call that message consistency. And well, this is where we learn our lesson.

Great brands and products typically have one singular mission. They don't waver. They don't waffle. They aren't wishy-washy. However you define it, they stick to their message and consistently deliver it to their audience in every form possible. Whether it's TV, digital, print, radio, outdoor, conferences/events, social media, sponsorships and more, successful brands stay on message regardless of the channel. They also spend a lot more to make their message clear to the consumer than the "two dollars ... cash" the paperboy in *Better Off Dead* demanded from Lane Meyer. In fact, brands are poised to spend almost $700 billion annually in 2019[1] to give you the Inigo Montoya messaging treatment.

---

1 https://www.marketingcharts.com/advertising-trends/spending-and-spenders-107665

*Great brands and products typically
have one singular mission. They
don't waver. They don't waffle.*

★ **Be clear.**

Successful brands with long-term viability are also honest in their messaging. Gone are the days of Lucky Strike cigarettes telling you, "To keep a slender figure no one can deny...Reach for a Lucky" or "For Digestion's Sake...Smoke Camels" or how about all the way back in 1921 when Listerine claimed that it cured everything from extreme dandruff to colds and could even be used as an after-shave tonic?[2] Now, this isn't to say that some brands haven't been caught up in a little fibbing recently, but in today's world, they usually pay substantially in reputation, stock price, credibility, legal fees and class action settlements. As the Thompson Twins said in the song "Lies" in 1983:

"You say you'll try harder
But I think it's just too late
Well, the car is revving in the drive,
And I'm not the sort to wait."

And that is exactly how your current customer and your target audience will view your brand if you stretch the truth or lack transparency in your messaging and advertising. Large global brands will sometimes get a second chance. You most likely will not. **Be honest.**

---

2   http://mentalfloss.com/article/20481/6-cases-shamelessly-false-advertising

Large global brands will sometimes get a second chance. You most likely will not. **Be honest.**

Inigo admits he's not professionally trained in sword fighting and he most certainly is not proficient in the arts of the assassin. I, on the other hand, watched every '80s ninja movie — *Enter the Ninja, American Ninja, Revenge of the Ninja, American Ninja 2, Nine Deaths of the Ninja, American Ninja 3* — and owned several throwing stars (Shuriken if you must know the Ninja name), Nunchuks and a blow-dart gun, so yeah I was pretty much a blue checkmark verified assassin. Nary a pillow or couch cushion could survive my stealthy yet furious attack.

So back to Inigo. Even though he was unknown in the assassin world and hadn't quite proved himself as a fighter, he still believed enough in himself to proudly and loudly state his mission. He did what is called today "breaking through the clutter," and he had the confidence to stand out regardless of his lack of real-life experience. We've seen examples of this with some iconic brands that were a little light on the market exposure when they took a big, bold chance. Brands like Monster. com who confidently spent $4 million dollars (almost their entire annual ad budget) on two 30-second spots during the 1999 NFL Championship Football Game in an effort to introduce their brand to the world.[3] "When I Grow Up" is still one of the most memorable spots in television history, and it squarely placed Monster.com as the preeminent online job search site in the world literally overnight. The spot was filmed in black and white and showed kids dressed for different lines of work

---

3   https://www.entrepreneur.com/article/173874

— businessperson, farmer, etc. — and saying things like "when I grow up, I want to file all day" and "when I grow up, I want to be underappreciated" and "I want to be a yes man, a yes woman." It ends with a question on the screen — "What did you want to be?" — and then the logo for Monster.com with a tagline that says *There's a better job out there*. More recently in 2013, Jamie Siminoff, founder of Ring.com, went on *Shark Tank* asking for $700,000 for 10% of his fledgling security company.[4] He boldly turned down an offer to invest from Mr. Wonderful because he didn't think it was fair and ultimately walked away with nothing. Fast forward five years when Amazon purchased his company for somewhere between $1.2 billion and $1.8 billion.[5]

Like Inigo, both Monster.com and Ring.com had confidence in their singular mission. Also like Inigo — who lacked the real-world experience using the skill he would need to back up his boldness — they also lacked some of the real-world experience with their product on a large scale that most would have believed necessary to reach the lofty heights they desired. If not for their bold action, it's likely that they would not have a prime bar stool at *Cheers* "where everybody knows your **brand** name" getting drinks from Sam Malone and Coach.

> *Like Inigo, both Monster.com and Ring.com had confidence in their singular mission.*

---

4   https://www.cnbc.com/2018/03/05/mark-cuban-on-shark-tank-reject-ring.html

5   https://www.cnbc.com/2018/02/27/amazon-buys-ring-the-smart-door-bell-maker-it-backed-through-alexa-fund.html

Whether it's your business or your career, it can be scary to go out on a limb and take a bold position. In the case of your business, it may require funds that you had set aside for something else, or it may mean incurring some debt in time, resources and possibly money without really knowing if you can actually pull it off when the time comes to prove yourself. But isn't that one of the reasons that you decided to be your own boss and start your own business? So you could call the shots, decide the strategy, and know that the belief in yourself was all the acknowledgment you would ever need. Of course, people could tell you that you're crazy (I'm sure as an entrepreneur you hear that all the time) but no boss or manager could stand in your way and tell you "No, you can't do that. It's too bold or too different or too aggressive."

If you are working for someone else and building your career, think about all the times you've heard someone say, "Interesting idea, but we aren't quite ready for that yet." Or "Why would we try that? We've always done it this way..." In the corporate world, bold can be scary to a lot of people. The status quo is the safe play, and most people are cool keeping their head just below the water's surface, thinking that once you've made yourself visible, you've also made yourself accountable. But isn't that what we should strive for? To be visible. Making a bold statement, presenting a bold idea or creating a bold solution?

Great companies and leaders encourage their employees to go big and rather than asking you to be the status quo, they ask you to challenge it. Invention, growth and progress are all a result of people who take the dare and go big sometimes without knowing if they can actually win the battle with the man "who killed their father." But if you are willing to "boldly go where no man has gone before" (yes, I know, not entirely '80s but it spans six decades one of which is the '80s, so I say it fits) you might be surprised just how far it can take you. Perhaps you, too, will find a "strange new world, new life or new civilization." And that is all the Star Trek I have in me. Nothing more. I promise.

> *Great companies and leaders encourage their*
> *employees to go big and rather than asking you*
> *to be the status quo, they ask you to challenge it.*

In the end, none of us — whether business owner or employee — wants to see our competitors do something bold that leads to success and then have to say, "Man, I wish we would have done that." **Be bold.**

Learn to say "no."

When we first meet our protagonist Westley, also known as the Man in Black, he is a young farm boy answering to every whim and need of Buttercup who he loves and adores. So much so that any time she asks him to do something, he says, "As you wish" — three words that ultimately go down in the love story annuls of movie history. From a purely romantic perspective, the idea of someone enamored enough with another to answer their requests with "As you wish" is the stuff of fairytales. Or if you are like me, it's the stuff of nightmares — like Freddie Krueger or Michael Myers nightmares.

So, let's assume that most people are normal and would enjoy this type of romantic gesture. If you are on the receiving side of this equation, it could be quite delightful and would certainly make many areas of your life much easier. If you are; however, the one fulfilling the wishes you might eventually get to the point where it could be overwhelming and potentially affect your ability to get the things done that you need to do for yourself. Eventually, you will have to make decisions on where to put your energy, meaning that some requests will only get partially done. At the same time, there is a very good chance that the quality of your tasks will diminish considerably, and mistakes will most certainly increase.

Not exactly a recipe for a happy ending.

Now let's switch Westley and Buttercup to manager and employee or boss and direct report or team leader and team member. You choose. At some point in our careers, most of us will be in the unenviable position of having to juggle more projects and requests than the number of '80s movies that starred Kevin Bacon, John Cusack or Patrick Swayze (it's 39, and you should watch all of them). To make matters worse; you've been given timelines that are as realistic as parachute pants making a fashion comeback. In fact, maybe this is where you are right now, and you are wondering how you are going to appease everyone's request.

Since I've been there before my guess is that you got to this place by saying "As you wish" each time you were asked to take on a new project or task. It's normal to want to say yes to work requests, particularly when they are coming from your manager or boss, and you are at the beginning of your career or vying for a promotion. It looks good on the surface, and you quickly become the go-to person. Everyone counts on you to deliver, and pretty soon you find yourself overwhelmed choosing between missing deadlines and missing out on life. All because you didn't take Nancy Reagan's advice to "just say no." And no doesn't mean can't. Can't is a bad and toxic word in the workplace. Can't is final. Can't is Cameron Frye before he is forced by his friend Ferris to have a good time.

> **And no doesn't mean can't. Can't is a bad and toxic word in the workplace. Can't is final. Can't is Cameron Frye before he is forced by his friend Ferris to have a good time.**

The word "no" does sound harsh, but it's the way that you say no that can make it sound substantially better than "can't," and sometimes the word itself isn't even necessary. Here's an example. You are buried in deliverables, and the stress is eating away at you like a Kiefer Sutherland *Lost Boy* vampire from Santa Carla when Dave the Delegator shows up at your desk:

Dave the Delegator: "Hey, I need your help with something. Should be a pretty easy project for you and I've got a really quick turnaround."

You (Internally and in your best Drago [the villain from Rocky IV] voice): "If he dies, he dies."

You (Externally): "Sounds great. I'd love to help. Currently, I'm on deadline with several projects for Bossman Benson, and then I'm working with Manager MaryBeth Lacey on a deliverable for Client Chewbacca. Once those are complete, I'd be happy to help. If you need it sooner, I'd ask that you speak with Bossman Benson or Manager Marybeth Lacey and see if they would be willing to move their project back to make room for yours."

Essentially, you've just said no and, even better, you've put the onus on Dave the Delegator to resolve his situation. Now if you find yourself having to do this with multiple people and on a frequent basis, then it's probably time to have an honest conversation with your manager about your workload and the challenges you are facing. If he or she is a good leader, they will work with you on a resolution or handle it with the team, but it is up to you to communicate.

And if you have direct reports or are running a business, it's very easy to continue to task your best person or people with the most important and deadline-driven projects. After all, they deliver for you consistently, and they have that "as you wish" mentality. But you may not know that they feel overburdened, stressed or frustrated until they drop their two weeks on your desk. They may be driven, but they are also human. The burden is on you to open up a line of communication and be cognizant of how you distribute the workload amongst the team; otherwise, your Westley may pursue a more enlightened Princess Buttercup. It is most certainly not "*inconceivable.*"

> ***The burden is on you to open up a line of communication and be cognizant of how you distribute the workload amongst the team; otherwise, your Westley may pursue a more enlightened Princess Buttercup.***

CHAPTER 3

CADDYSHACK

"Be the ball."

Ty Webb, *Caddyshack*

Like most sports, golf can teach us a lot of lessons in life but when you add the foursome of Chevy Chase, Bill Murray, Ted Knight and Rodney Dangerfield you might get a little more than you bargained for. *Caddyshack* is one of the greatest comedies of all time and a hilarious look inside what is likely a typical country club of the early '80s. The judge, the doctor, the priest, the trust fund baby, the blue-collar multi-millionaire, the goofy greenskeeper and the eclectic pack of caddies were like a group from the Island of the Misfit Toys and perhaps a parallel to those that inhabit so many workplaces.

The golf course presents a lot of unique challenges just as our career can, and when Ty played by Chevy Chase tells Danny the caddy who is struggling with his path in life to "be the ball" he is really telling him to take control of his own situation. In the workplace, we are often faced with the same dilemma, whether it is common like a project decision or more life-changing like the decision to take a new job. You ultimately need to **trust your gut, trust your judgment and trust yourself.** That first bit of advice worked for *Magnum P.I.* in every episode, so it should work just fine for you as well.

Trust.

Such a small word with such potentially huge implications. Because we know ourselves better than anyone else, it tends to be easy to trust ourselves. Sometimes too easy. In the workplace, we often miss what the goofy greenskeeper in *Caddyshack* — Carl Spackler — called the "Cinderella story." This is a person who comes out of nowhere to solve a problem or provide ideas for moving forward on a struggling project. We are so busy being worried about our accountability that we can find ourselves being distrustful of people's motives and abilities. *Meet the Parents* was most certainly not an '80s movie (so forgive me for this immortal sin) but Jack Byrnes's "circle of trust" is a very real thing and too often we only allow one person in it: ourselves. So much of our work stress and inefficiencies can be eliminated when we realize that **solutions can come from anyone when we are willing to expand our circle of trust.**

> *In the workplace, we often miss what the goofy greenskeeper in* **Caddyshack** *— Carl Spackler — called the "Cinderella story."*

Before we tee off and learn what our country clubbers from *Caddyshack* can teach us about the workplace, let's go all *Time Bandits* and follow our time-traveling dwarves back to July of 1980.

It was July of 1980, and I was a month away from celebrating my 10th birthday while outfitted in super short OP corduroy shorts, a bowl cut and striped tube socks pulled up to my bony knees. Stud life. Yes, I spent those Richard Marx-style "Endless Summer Nights" catching fireflies and playing ghost in the graveyard, kick the can and Marco Polo. *So* much stud life. And the days? Well, the days were complete crazy town — riding our Green Machines up and down the block while pelting each other with crabapples.

Of course, my summer of '80 story would be incomplete without mentioning that I attended my first rock concert that year. That's right and front row to boot. Everyone jamming together and creating a ruckus that Principal Vernon would be proud of. Okay, that's a lie as it's hard to create a ruckus while singing along to Air Supply. Yup. My first concert was Air Supply at the county fair with my mom. And, yes, I was absolutely dragged there, kicking and screaming. To this day, I can still hear her singing at the front of the stage, *"I'm all out of love. I'm so lost without you. I know you were right believing for so long."* Seared into my brain.

Years later, she would sing along to House of Pain in the car — *"I came to get down. I came to get down. So, get out your seat and jump around"* — a little redemption, I suppose. Maybe.

Speaking of music, we were once again blessed with an insane variety on the billboard charts. The aforementioned *Air Supply* added another to the list of shower-singing break up songs with "All out of Love," while on the completely opposite side of the spectrum, *Ted Nugent* debuted "Wango Tango" to the delight of many mullet and Levi jean jacket-wearing Camaro drivers. The S.O.S Band provided a heartbeat to disco and leisure suits with "Take your Time (Do it Right)" and one of the master musical storytellers of all time, Billy Joel hit number #1 with "It's Still Rock and Roll to Me."

On Television, CNN began officially broadcasting 24-hours news in late June of 1980 while Cinemax launched its 24-hour movie channel on August 1st to the delight of many a teenage boy (or night owls). We said goodbye to one of my dad's favorites, *The Rockford Files* and were thoroughly entertained by Robin Williams in the middle of his *Mork and Mindy* run. We also had the sport of the future beamed straight into our living rooms with the weekly excitement of the *Professional Bowlers Tour.* So, when you complain about having too many channels with nothing on, just think about that for a minute and get back to me. Regularly scheduled broadcasted Bowling. Wow.

FUN FACT: ABC Network's Saturday PBA (Pro Bowling Association) telecasts posted a Nielsen rating of 8.5, beating out golf, tennis and basketball. Yes, the '80s were a different time in so many ways.

At the box office, *The Empire Strikes Back* was completing
two months in the top three while *Cheech and Chong's Next
Movie* — with a similar special effects budget — continued
to smoke their way to success. One of the most underrated
films of the decade in my humble opinion, *My Bodyguard* (no
not the one with Kevin Costner and Whitney Houston) was
drawing in a consistent audience. It starred Chris Makepeace of
Meatballs fame, Adam Baldwin and a young Matt Dillon — its
lessons on bullying were way ahead of their time. "I am serious
and don't call me Shirley" was just one of many quotes from
Airplane that have continued on in the American lexicon as it
was beginning a run that continues even today.

And then, of course, we had our beloved, and oft-quoted
Caddyshack. Opening on July 25th, 1980 it was directed by
Harold Ramis who you might know as Dr. Egon Spengler from
Ghostbusters which he also co-wrote. The cast was a who's who
of comedy genius with Chevy Chase, Bill Murray, Ted Knight
and Rodney Dangerfield and the result was in a word: magnificent. The story is pretty simple, but it is the delivery and
chemistry of everyone involved that takes it to historical status.
Caddyshack is set in the late 70s/early '80s and takes us through
the typical and atypical days and evenings of an uppity country
club that is comprised of many colorful characters (I do love
my alliteration). Characters like Ty Webb (Chevy Chase) the
wealthy player (in the bachelor sense) who fashions himself
a philosopher, Judge Smails (Ted Knight), the prototypical
country club snob, (Rodney Dangerfield), the multi-millionaire
man of the people who brings a working man's perspective to
the club and lives to annoy the bourgeois set — who actually
sounds like he would be pretty close to the real Dangerfield —
and groundskeeper (Bill Murray) who spends his days plotting

the demise of a single gopher that is determined to destroy the course while making a mockery of everyone.

FUN FACT: Grande Oaks, a golf club in Davie, FL was the setting for Bushwood country club, and Judge Smails's house — where he kicks Danny out after catching him with his niece — is located on the golf course at Coral Ridge Country Club in Ft. Lauderdale, FL.

Caddyshack is an ensemble cast with every standard country club personality represented, including a few that will provide us with our lessons for this chapter. The plot has several storylines all interconnected in some way, and all designed to bring out the funny. And it delivers. From an end-of-the-world, panic-inducing Baby Ruth candy bar floating in a pool to the slice heard 'round Bushwood to the classic "Cinderella story" — two words that have probably been said in at least 46 offices and 24 golf courses since I started this paragraph — almost every scene brings something quotable for generations to come.

So, what does our colorful group of country club members, employees and a ninja-like gopher teach us about today's workplace?

 Trust your gut. Trust your judgment. Trust yourself.

As you are reading this, you may be in a situation where you are struggling with an important business or project decision. Wrangling and wavering back and forth in your head. Justifying every move that keeps you thinking and evaluating, rather than taking action. Maybe even like the scene in *Animal House*, you have the angel on one shoulder and the devil on the other. Any way you define it, you're stuck. Maybe you can't see the right path or maybe the path is blocked in your head or maybe there are way too many in front of you, and you've convinced yourself that only one leads to the answer, solution or success. It's a lonely place to be, and it makes your stomach churn. Guess what? You aren't alone. Just look down the street at the other businesses or across the hall in another office or peer into the next office building and you can be assured that there are people just like you engaged in the same individual battle.

When Ty Webb, played by Chevy Chase, says *"I'm going to give you a little advice. There's a force in the universe that makes things happen. And all you have to do is get in touch with it, stop thinking, let things happen, and be the ball",* he is speaking with Danny, a caddie, at Bushwood. The conversation takes place while they are on the course by themselves talking about all things life with the occasional faux Buddhist Zen lesson from Ty.

Danny is struggling with where he wants his life to go and what path he should take. Certainly not unusual for someone in their late teens or early 20s but Danny doesn't have the luxuries of life like the club members with their money and opportunity. He works as a caddy to earn money for college and begins to realize that his dreams of a law school education are further and further away. He's desperate. So much so that he attempts to schmooze the uber-obnoxious Judge Smails. who grants a scholarship each year. Danny does this by informing the judge that he wants to attend law school, but his parents don't have the money. To which Judge Smails so eloquently replies, "Well, the world needs ditch diggers, too."

Danny decides to ignore what is perhaps the most blatant hammer-in-the-face insult in movie history and continue his march down desperation street with his ongoing attempts to woo the insufferable Judge. He sounds like the male half of Human League's 1981 hit song "Don't You Want Me?" completely forgetting his conversation with Ty about being the ball. Rather than letting things happen by trusting himself and the "force in the universe," he locks in on a potential opportunity that will require substantial groveling at best and sheer self-degradation at worst. This is what can happen to us in the workplace when we lose our confidence — even if for just a moment — and stop trusting our gut, our judgment and ultimately ourselves. We end up in a situation where an outcome that is our responsibility is now out of our control and in the hands of someone who we have given undeserved power. In most cases, they know it.

> *We end up in a situation where an outcome that is our responsibility is now out of our control and in the hands of someone who we have given undeserved power. In most cases, they know it.*

Even if you are the ultimate decision-maker and you don't have the concern that most do of conceding the power of a decision to someone for the wrong reasons, you may still find yourself struggling to find the right path or solution. As we discussed above, you've begun wavering, waffling and wrangling (there's that amazing alliteration again…and again). You've lost your mojo and along with it your confidence to make the right decision. We study spreadsheets, analytics and sometimes more data in a week than any human should consume in a lifetime. The very tools that were supposed to help us be more efficient and more accurate are now causing us to overthink in what is referred to as paralysis by analysis.

When leaders consistently overthink decisions, it can lead to an environment where your team members feel stuck, innovation slows and growth stagnates. Great leaders know when it is time to trust their gut, follow their instincts, and "be the ball."

You may slice a few. You may hook a few. You may even have to yell "Fore!" to avoid an awkward apology, but when you do stripe it right down the middle of the fairway, the results will be, in the words of Jeff Spicoli, "Awesome! Totally Awesome!"

 Solutions can come from anyone. Expand your circle of trust.

One of the more popular buzz phrases these days is "stay in your lane." Now if you've read my first book, you know that I despise buzzwords, buzz phrases and most of all that purveyor of all things ridiculous — Buzzword Bob — who unfortunately inhabits every office across our planet. Having said that, I've been guilty of embracing the idea of staying in your lane. Really you say? The Eeyore of buzzwords actually embraced one? Yes. Yes, I did and let me explain. If you've ever been in marketing, worked in a creative department or spent time at an ad agency, then you've had to deal with every Tom, Dick and Sally coming at you with their "expert" opinion on your logo, ad campaign or image. Actually, they typically provide their input on anything creative. I mean after all; they did watch every single NFL Championship Football game ad and even rated them on a website the day after.

Now I can't speak for every other department, but I do wonder if the same people have an opinion on the number of columns on the latest accounting spreadsheet or the applied discounts in the latest purchasing agreement. Doubtful. It's the visual aspects of marketing and advertising that attract everyone's attention and input. I mean those of us who do creative for a living know how cool it is when you can point to something in public and say, "I did that." At the very least, you can say you played a part in the creation. Tom, Dick and Sally are no different and as frustrating as it can be when their critique is less than constructive, sometimes a fresh set of eyes is exactly what is needed. Asking someone for their opinion or feedback who is outside of the artificial, fictional and often selfishly isolated center-of-the-solution universe inside of your business can provide you with the answers that have been eluding the team. You might be surprised where the best insights reside within the company and who knows, the next great leader could be the one person who everyone overlooks because of their position or experience. You could say that they came "outta nowhere." And Tom, Dick and Sally, as much as you might think it, we are not talking about you.

When Carl Spackler (played by Bill Murray), our dimwitted and lovable greenskeeper and part-time gopher hunter says *"Cinderella story. Outta nowhere. A former greenskeeper, now about to become the Masters champion,"* he is swinging a golf club using the tops of flowers as the ball right in front of the club entrance. Like most of us do from time to time, he is daydreaming, except his dream involves doing some slight damage to his employer's landscaping.

 DIGRESSION ALERT: often we hear that daydreaming is just for kids and that we should grow out of it. Hogwash, as my grandfather used to say. Never send your imagination away to a place where it can't be accessed because people without dreams told you that you should. Embrace your inner Peter Pan and allow yourself time to continue believing that anything is possible. You may just find that it unlocks the answer to a business question that has been stumping you. At the very least, you'll remember how it felt when you looked at every day with wonder and curiosity and what it was like when the word impossible wasn't in your vocabulary.

For those of you who aren't off daydreaming somewhere, let's get back to Carl the greenskeeper and what he taught us. To put into perspective how he was perceived by the club members and people in general, let's use my favorite piece of dialogue from the movie. Ty Webb an eccentric club member (played by Chevy Chase) is practicing his golf game at night when he hits a stray shot into the grounds crew building that houses all the landscape equipment. Unbeknownst to Ty, this is also Carl's home. At one point during their conversation, Carl says they should hang out sometime and Ty, being a nice guy, says, "Sure, come on over anytime," which then leads to this:

Carl: "You have a pool?"

Ty: "We have a pond in the back. We have a pool and a pond. The pond would be good for you."

Yes, this is the life of Carl, the greenskeeper, but regardless of his station in life, he continues to stay positive and dream big. When he places himself in the position to be the "Cinderella story" and win the Masters championship, we laugh at the ridiculousness of it all as we should. I mean, this is the same guy who blows up half the golf course trying to win a movie-long battle against a gopher who ultimately wins and does a victory dance to a Kenny Loggins song.

But in the workplace, we have the potential for Cinderella stories all around us. Oftentimes, leaders are so laser-focused on the team in front of them or the people with the "right titles" that they miss the Masters champions in the making. We have to look beyond that circle of trust we've created and seek out ideas, opinions and feedback from the people who may not be in a position that typically requires their inclusion in the process. It could be an intern, an administrative assistant, the person who cleans the office at night or even the office introvert who rarely speaks up and reminds you of the Ally Sheedy character in *The Breakfast Club*. Any of them could come from "outta nowhere" and provide the breakthrough needed or a fresh idea that could take a project in a new and positive direction. They just need someone to give them the chance to bring "a hush over the crowd" and be the Cinderella story.

Be that leader that gives everyone that chance.

And if you are the one who has ideas but needs the opportunity to share them, then take this wisdom nugget from the eccentric club member Ty Webb who says to Danny: *"See your future. Be your future. Make your future."*

Go make that future. I know I am.

CHAPTER 4

FAST TIMES AT RIDGEMONT HIGH

"I like that ... I don't know. That's nice."

Mr. Hand, *Fast Times at Ridgemont High*

Believe it or not, there are a number of parallels between high school and the workplace. Some good, like teamwork and personal growth. Others not so good, like cliques and gossip. The student body at Ridgemont High School back in 1982, delivered examples of each, but going beyond these surface lessons is where the core of our education for this chapter can be found. As Hall and Oates said in their 1985 hit song, "Adult Education" — "What you want is an adult education," and yes Jeff Spicoli is actually going to deliver that to you.

Fast Times at Ridgemont High introduced us to a familiar face for the first time — Mr. Hand. Although none of us had

technically met Mr. Hand, I say familiar because he epito-
mized the '80s high school teacher who had little time to suffer
fools which meant he had very little time for Spicoli. At one
point early in the movie, Spicoli is tardy once again, and when
asked why he can't make it to class on time, he simply says,
"I don't know." For some reason, even thinking about saying
those three words in the workplace has somehow become
synonymous with weakness and lack of preparation or worse,
lack of intelligence. But as we will find out, **it is okay to say,**
"I don't know" and in fact, one can and will argue that it is
a more a sign of strength and character than anything negative.
Of course, using that response when you are tardy to work is
not advised.

More and more, we are hearing about toxic work environments
and toxic leadership. Toxic is not a word that you ever wanted
associated with you or your company unless it's followed by the
word avenger as in the 1984 Troma Entertainment cult classic,
The Toxic Avenger. And even then, maybe not so much. As we
now know, when employees do leave, they are usually leaving
their manager or the company and not the job.

When Spicoli was trying to explain an integral and historical
step in the building of America and said, "So what Jefferson was
saying was 'Hey! You know, we left this England place because
it was bogus. So, if we don't get some cool rules ourselves,
pronto, we'll just be bogus too,'" he was actually onto something in today's workplace. In the past, the employer typically
had the upper hand and leverage over the loyal employee who
would stay for 25 years; that is if they were lucky enough to
avoid a layoff. And even if they did make it through the first
downsizing, they would eventually be moved out and given

the proverbial gold watch as a thank you. Now, with the ability to find a new job literally at your fingertips, increased competition, an incredibly mobile workforce with options to also work remotely and the increased acceptance of what used to be called "job hopping" the one-sided loyalty advantage that employers enjoyed is virtually gone. This is a very good thing, and this is also why **striving to make your place of business the greatest and coolest place to work** is an absolute necessity in today's environment and really should be built into every business plan.

Finally, in the category of what Culture Club called "Karma Chameleon" back in 1984, Spicoli will unwittingly teach us that **when ordering lunch in the office, always make sure to get enough for everyone.**

Now, before we learn more about what Spicoli, Mr. Hand and the student body at Ridgemont High taught us about today's workplace let's very carefully hop in the time machine with the "I'll be back" cyborg known as *The Terminator* and pay a visit to 1982.

It was August of 1982, and I was moving quickly toward my 12th birthday. The last one, before my incredibly awkward teenage years. Ha, who am I kidding? I was already awkward considering that I was all of 5'5 with size-13 shoes on my feet and feathered hair that would put Keith Partridge, Rick Springfield and Leif Garrett all to shame. So yeah, I was pretty much a human duck. That was a fun time.

Thankfully awkward-looking 11-year-olds could find respite in the mall and boardwalk arcades of yore, and I was no exception. The early '80s were the golden years of arcade games, and in 1982 we were introduced to names like Dig Dug, Joust and Q*bert, all of which had no problem separating me from the quarters that I worked so hard to locate under the family room couch cushions and in the dryer. As I reflect back, it's pretty incredible how much "joy and pain" (see what I did there, Rob Base and DJ E-Z Rock?) one single quarter could produce once it was dropped into the slot next to the 25¢ insignia backlit in standard arcade red. Speaking of Rob Base and DJ E-Z Rock, the summer of 1982 was also my first introduction to hip hop in the form of the song "Planet Rock" by Afrika Bambaataa & The Soul Sonic Force. It was actually released in April of that year, but without the luxury of the internet to send things to us at flux-capacitor speed, it sometimes took a bit until you actually got to hear the really groundbreaking stuff.

And as it was wont to do in the '80s, the Top 40 during August of 1982 was providing us with a plethora of sounds some of which are having a second bite at the big red shiny apple of fame here in the 2000s. "Don't You Want Me" by The Human League was sitting at #10 and was most recently used in a Walmart commercial in 2018. "Tainted Love" by Soft Cell was at #17 and has been used numerous times in commercials including a classic M&Ms spot in 2015.

Sitting atop the billboard charts was perhaps one of the most iconic workout songs of all time, as "Eye of the Tiger" was in its third straight week at #1.

DIGRESSION ALERT: Mr. T as Clubber Lang in *Rocky, III,* **which is where the song "Eye of the**

Tiger" premiered, is one of my favorite movie characters of all time.

Finally, and bringing flashbacks from one of the most embarrassing moments in my youth (the Air Supply concert with my mom mentioned in Chapter 3), the guys in Air Supply were holding down the #7 spot with "Even the Nights Are Better." Ugh.

On TV, we were ending our first summer without laughs from two of the soon-to-be biggest stars in Hollywood history as *Bosom Buddies* with Tom Hanks and *Mork & Mindy* with Robin Williams came to an end the prior spring. But not to worry as we were being thoroughly entertained by Higgins, TC, Rick and one of the best mustaches to grace the screen in *Magnum P.I.* We were laughing at the antics of three single roommates (I still miss John Ritter) and their landlord in *Three's Company* and laughing even harder at Sherman Hemsley and Isabel Sanford as they moved on up in *The Jeffersons*.

 FUN FACT: Tom Selleck was the first choice for Indiana Jones in the first *Raiders of the Lost Ark* but his contract with *Magnum P.I.* kept him from accepting the role.

In terms of any substantial TV premieres, it was pretty much as barren as the Sahara desert which was disappointing but as Christian Slater said in *The Heathers*, "Well, everybody's life has got static." Then, in the words of Pat Benatar, TV "hit us with its best shot" and we had 12 weeks of amazing with the premieres of *Family Ties, Cheers* (such a great ending — "Sorry, we're closed"), *St. Elsewhere* and the German rock star and his talking car, *Knight Rider.* Just thinking about all of these shows brings me right back to my family room as a kid playing board games like Candy Land, Chutes and Ladders, and Life.

At the box office, Jason donned his infamous hockey mask for the third time in *Friday the 13th Part III* and slashed his way straight to #1 thus knocking our lost and gentle alien *E.T.* (who taught us about social responsibility in my 1st book — yes, that's called a shameless plug) down to the #2 spot. Steven Spielberg was turning the static from a late-night TV into the definition for demonic possession in *Poltergeist* and one of the most underrated comedies of all time and one which I highly recommend, *Night Shift,* was having moderate success at the box office. Directed by Ron Howard of Opie fame and starring Henry Winkler, Michael Keaton and Shelly Long, it had a soundtrack that contained songs from The Pointer Sisters, Rod Stewart, Marshall Crenshaw and Chaka Khan. It also had one of the iconic '80s songs "Talk, Talk" by well...Talk Talk. So, yeah, you need to put this movie on your list today. Like now. Go do it. Seriously.

 FUN FACT: If you still need another reason to put *Night Shift* on your list, you'll get to see Kevin Costner in one of his classic roles as "Frat Boy #1." It's always cool to see the great ones in their early roles.

And then we had what many consider to be "the '80s movie of '80s movies" as *Fast Times at Ridgemont High* hit the box office on August 13, 1982, which we can assume was a very warm late summer Friday evening. It was directed by Amy Heckerling, who also wrote and directed *Clueless* (amongst others), and was written by Cameron Crowe, who wrote and directed *Say Anything* (amongst others). And the cast? Well, as *Bill and Ted* and a guitar riff said, it was "Excellent!" Just take a look at this list — Sean Penn, Judge Reinhold, Phoebe Cates (wow), Jennifer Jason Leigh, Eric Stoltz, Forest Whitaker, Anthony Edwards, Taylor Negron and one Nicholas Coppola (who later became Nicholas Cage). Oh, and one of the great '80s female power rockers, Nancy Wilson from the band Heart, had a cameo as the "beautiful girl in car."

Fast Times is a coming-of-age movie that told the story of one totally righteous high school in early '80s California and the students that populated its hallways. Cameron Crowe actually went undercover in 1981 to do the research for his book that the movie is based on which follows a number of characters as they navigate their way through the school year. You had the stoner surfer crew of Nicholas Cage, Anthony Edwards and Eric Stoltz, all led by one Jeff Spicoli (whose bobblehead is sitting on my desk and staring at me while I write this) played magnificently by Sean Penn. Of all the incredible characters from '80s movies, Spicoli may be the most iconic and the one that continues to be integrated into popular culture generation after generation. As an example, there is a raw bar near my house — Papa's Rawbar — that I frequent and a staff member in his early 20s is nick-named Spicoli — it fits. Those who gave him his nickname and the kid himself weren't even born until the 1990s; so, yes it looks as though our favorite surfer dude will live on forever. Hmmm ... maybe he's a Highlander.

Beyond Spicoli, there is Bradley Hamilton (played by Judge Reinhold), who is one of the more popular kids and whose pride and joy is both his 1960 Buick LeSabre and his younger sister, Stacy, played by Jennifer Jason Leigh. Stacy works at the Pizza Parlor in the local mall and is a quiet and shy high school sophomore while her best friend, Linda Barrett, played by Phoebe Cates, is the exact opposite. There's Damone, the wannabe ladies' man and ticket scalper, and his friend Mark Ratner, who is the male version of Stacy with an added dose of teenage insecurity. As a bonus, we are treated to a few scenes with the incredibly talented Forest Whitaker who plays Charles Jefferson the Ridgemont High football star and the legendary Ray Walston who plays Mr. Hand and will teach us one of our lessons later in this chapter.

FUN FACTS: Sean Penn was hired for the part of Spicoli after a short chat prior to his audition, which then became unnecessary. Judge Reinhold was the upstairs neighbor of the director, Amy Heckerling and ultimately got the part of Brad. And Nicolas Coppola who auditioned for the part of Brad but ultimately landed the part of "Brad's bud" is the nephew of Francis Ford Coppola and is now known as Nicolas Cage. Did you follow that? Good. Oh and Mark Ratner? Well his character was based on a student from the high school (Clairemont HS in San Diego) where Crowe went undercover to do research for

a non-fiction book. That student was Andy Rathbone, who went on to write many of the "For Dummies" series of books about computer programs.[1]

All these characters take us on a hilarious and sometimes serious trip through those awkward formative high school years that no one escapes. And when you allow Amy Heckerling and Cameron Crowe the creative freedom to bring it all together, the end result is historic genius. Don't believe me? Well, *Fast Times* was selected for preservation by the Library of Congress and inducted into the US National Film Registry in 2006 — so, yeah historic.

But what did our cast of Ridgemont high school characters teach us about today's workplace?

It's okay to say, "I don't know."

From the first time they meet, Mr. Hand, who teaches history at Ridgemont High, and Spicoli have a complex relationship. Spicoli is late on his first day of class and Mr. Hand doesn't take truancy lightly, as we find out when he rips up Spicoli's schedule card and throws the pieces on the floor — to which Spicoli says, "Hey, you're ripping my card."

The next time they interact, Spicoli is late once again, but this time he is brought to class by another student who Mr.

---

1   https://www.ifc.com/2014/10/15-things-you-probably-didnt-know-about-fast-times-at-ridgemont-high

Hand has sent out to find him. He has a bagel tucked in the top of his jeans, with his shirt open and when Mr. Hand asks him the reason for his truancy, Spicoli responds with "Just couldn't make it on time." The conversation continues, which leads us to this classic exchange that will be the premise for this lesson:

> **Mr. Hand**: "Why are you continuously late for this class, Mr. Spicoli? Why do you shamelessly waste my time like this?"
>
> **Spicoli**: "I don't know."

Mr. Hand then approaches the chalkboard and writes "I Don't Know" in big, bold letters and says: "I like that ... I don't know. That's nice."

He goes on to tell Spicoli that he is going to leave his words on the chalkboard for all of his classes to see and will give him full credit for them, to which Spicoli says, "Well, alright!"

It is one of many classic scenes in the movie, and the two of them together have great comedic chemistry. But when Spicoli provides that incredibly simplistic three-word answer of "I don't know" to Mr. Hand's question, it actually teaches us a very valuable lesson for the workplace.

How many times in the workplace have you been in a position where you are asked a question and truly do not know the answer? If your answer to this question is never, then in the words of Enid Strict (aka The Church Lady), "Well, isn't that special?" But if you're like most of us, you've experienced this on multiple occasions throughout your career and each time you probably paused longer than you might think as you raced through your head for some sort of answer that would satisfy the person asking (or, worse yet, the room full of your peers waiting for you to espouse your brilliance).

> **How many times in the workplace have you been in a position where you are asked a question and truly do not know the answer? If your answer to this question is never, then in the words of Enid Strict (aka The Church Lady), "Well, isn't that special?"**

So, you formulate what you think is a well-thought-out answer in the second or two that you have. Unfortunately, what you say comes out sounding more like Lloyd Dobler's rambling answer in the movie *Say Anything* (great lessons from this movie in my first book — another shameless plug) when Diane Court's father asks Lloyd what his plans are for the future, to which Lloyd replies:

"I've thought about this quite a bit, sir and I would have to say considering what's waiting out there for me ... I don't want to sell anything, buy anything, or process anything as a career. I don't want to sell anything bought or processed, or buy anything sold or processed, or process anything sold, bought, or processed, or repair anything sold, bought, or processed."

Rambling and a bit confusing without a real answer. But fortunately for Lloyd Dobler, he was super cool and could fall back on his kickboxing training (which he called "the sport of the future"). You and I aren't that lucky or that super cool. Well, maybe you are, but I'm not.

It's normal to want to answer the question that is directly asked
of you, especially when it's your manager or when it's in a room
full of your team members. All of us want to look our best at
work and be the one with the answers or the solutions to the
problem. As you are searching for the answer, you may start
talking just to fill the silence in the hopes that you will stumble
across it 20 or 30 words into your nervous attempt at stalling as
you say to yourself *c'mon, you got this ... think*! But what if you
don't have the answer? What if no matter what recess of your
brain you reach into, that *Magnum P.I.* "little voice inside you"
says you simply don't know?

Herein lies our lesson from Mr. Hand and the unforgettable Jeff
Spicoli. It really is okay to say, "I don't know." *What did he just
say*? Audible gasps can be heard coming from the room, and
then a hush falls over the crowd. Whispers permeate as conference chair neighbors lean into each other and quietly ask, "Did
he just admit that he didn't know? I mean, did he actually say,
'I don't know?'" Three words that have been treated as taboo in
the business world and viewed as a one-way ticket down the
corporate ladder. How dare you not be omnipotent? You should
be the equivalent of the all-knowing and all-seeing eye of the
three witches in the *Clash of the Titans* — the 1981 version, of
course, not the 2010 remake.

**DIGRESSION ALERT: If you are anything like me,
at this very moment you can hear them saying
"Give us the eye" to Perseus played by the dapper
Harry Hamlin.**

The idea that we should have all the answers at the time that someone asks a question is such an old-school approach to business and dare I say unrealistic. Furthermore, the idea that saying "I don't know" is a sign of vulnerability, weakness or that it implies you aren't proficient at your job is just plain silly. On the contrary, saying those three words is a sign of strength and confidence. Rather than attempting to make something up or take the Buzzword Bob approach and fill the space with, well, buzzwords, in the hopes that you can replicate the all-knowing eye, you've admitted that you are human. Oh, the horror!

Admitting that you don't know can also position as you as a leader in the eyes of your other team members. They will now look at you as the person who was unafraid to take a chance, by stepping up and paving the way for the rest of the team to deliver honestly and transparently. This relaxes everyone and frees people of the stress of feeling as if you need to have every answer or fabricate it when you don't. You know that burden that you carry when you know something isn't real, that you are faking it like Ronald Miller in the 1987 film *Can't Buy Me Love,* and that at some point it will eventually catch up to you.

I must, however, add a quick caveat here. When saying I don't know, it is good practice to include something like, "Let me look into it and get back to you," after those three words. Or "But I'll find the answer and get you the information." Although I believe strongly in the positive power of "I don't know," it doesn't stand up very well on its own and will be received much better with the idea that an answer or solution is forthcoming. After all, even Spicoli was able to muster an emphatic "Well, alright" to support his initial "I don't know."

And if your boss answers your "I don't know" with a retort of "I like that ... I don't know ...That's nice," well, maybe the way to that next promotion is an increased use of '80s movie quotes at work. I mean, once again, that would be in the words of Spicoli, "Awesome! Totally Awesome!"

Strive to make your place of business the greatest and coolest place to work.

On the surface, this lesson may sound obvious. Create a great place to work, and great employees will follow. I mean shouldn't this be common sense? You would think so, but there's a reason that each year, various publications feel compelled to share a list of "The best places to work." Typically, when you have to list the best of something, it usually means that there is a much larger category that represents the mediocre or the worst in the same group.

There's a point in the movie where Mr. Hand visits Spicoli at his house on prom night to deliver the news that he isn't going to pass his history class and will, therefore, have to repeat his senior year and not graduate. It is toward the end of the movie and represents the first time that we see Spicoli actually concerned and unsure of himself. Thankfully for him, Mr. Hand provides him with the opportunity to try and pass a verbal pop quiz, and one of the questions about Thomas Jefferson prompts this spectacular answer from Spicoli:

> *"What Jefferson was saying was, 'Hey! You know, we left this England place 'cause it was bogus; so if we don't get some cool rules ourselves — pronto — we'll just be bogus, too!' Get it?"*

I'm not sure that Mr. Hand actually did "get it," but he allowed Spicoli to pass and then off he went to celebrate prom in his checkered Vans, Hawaiian shirt and tie.

As ridiculous and hilarious as this statement is, it actually did teach us something incredibly valuable about the workplace today. How many times have you read something that says people don't quit their *jobs*, they quit their managers — that is to say they leave because of the way they are treated by their employer or manager or both? Separated by 100 plus years and 100 plus points in their IQs, Jeff Spicoli and Thomas Jefferson both recognized that a bogus environment would create a lack of trust, an eroding belief in the system and ultimately the loss of your best people.

> *Separated by 100 plus years and 100 plus points in their IQs, Jeff Spicoli and Thomas Jefferson both recognized that a bogus environment would create a lack of trust, an eroding belief in the system and ultimately the loss of your best people.*

Sometimes the offending company is simply unaware that, in the words of Tangina Barrons, who plays the ghost-seeing clairvoyant and psychic in the original *Poltergeist,* their "house is not clean." In the worst situations — the ones that we often hear about in the news via lawsuits or otherwise — the business has simply decided not to prioritize the creation of a healthy work environment or, in some instances, leadership is determined to foster a negative one. Other times it isn't anything nefarious or outwardly hostile in any way. It's just a lack of effort on the part of leadership to create a place where people enjoy coming to work and feel that the company values them through actions like great perks, recognition and the flexibility that a majority of people require in their jobs today. The fact that so many companies are still blind to the idea and practice of creating employee loyalty is, in the words of Vizzini in *The Princess Bride*, "Inconceivable!"

When a company grows, and especially when growth happens quickly, the environment evolves and finds its roots with the strongest personalities. If these personalities aren't guided by a simple, well-established and principled mission, then a bogus environment can rapidly become toxic. It's the responsibility of the leader at the top to set the tone and plant the seeds that will be the company's way forward. In Chapter 1, we learned a few very valuable lessons from *The Outsiders*, one of which was the idea of "staying gold" through the tough times in your business and your career. Companies that start with that idea in mind and build their principles around it will avoid the dreaded Spicoli bogus tag and thus thrive as they become a place where everyone aspires to work.

The good news is that more and more companies are beginning to understand this correlation and some organizations "get it" so much that they are consistently rated as one of the best places to work. Companies like Google, In-N-Out Burger, Southwest Airlines and Salesforce are just a few that consistently land on multiple lists of the best places to work. And because I make my home in South Florida, I also have to mention Ultimate Software and JM Family Enterprises, two South Florida-based companies that pride themselves on being recognized by a variety of national publications and websites as a best place to work year after year. With friends working at both places, I know firsthand that this award is well-deserved. Companies like these make me so proud of my adopted hometown.

No company will ever be perfect, and no matter how much they try, there will always be a few people whose experiences don't live up to the expectations coming in. I mean *Ferris Bueller's Day Off* only scored a 79% rating on Rotten Tomatoes, so you can't satisfy everyone even when you create one of the great pieces of 20th-century artwork. In this guy's very humble opinion, the best thing any business can do is prioritize building an amazing human resources (HR) team and make a clear investment in them. The CEO and leadership team should work with the HR department from the outset to develop a positive, rewarding and open atmosphere that starts from the minute a new employee walks through the door on their first day. Too many times, companies deprioritize HR, particularly in the area of employee retention. The impact this has on the ability of a business to grow and succeed, as well as the real dollar costs of employee turnover, is immeasurable.

Be "gold" not "bogus" and make your business or your team so "cool" that no one wants to leave your "England place." Get it? Great. So, in the words of that 1960 Buick LeSabre-loving, best-movie-big-bro-ever Bradley Hamilton, "*Learn it. Know it. Live it.*"

BONUS LESSON

Because we just have to laugh with Spicoli one last time,
I've slipped in a little bonus lesson to end our chapter. If
the lesson references Spicoli, then, of course, it must also
include Mr. Hand.

There is a moment in the movie when Spicoli arrives to class on
time and sits quietly and properly, which causes Mr. Hand to do
a double-take. During his lecture, there's a knock at the door by
a pizza delivery guy who drops off a pizza at Spicoli's desk right
in the middle of class.

FUN FACT: Pizza is spectacular.

This prompts **Mr. Hand** to say, "Am I hallucinating here? Just
what the hell do you think you're doing?" This then leads to the
classic exchange:

> **Spicoli**: "Learning about Cuba and having some food."

> **Mr. Hand**: "Mr. Spicoli, you're on dangerous ground here.
> You're causing a major disturbance on my time."

> **Spicoli**: "I've been thinking about this, Mr. Hand. If I'm here
> and you're here, doesn't that make it our time? Certainly,
> there's nothing wrong with a little feast on our time."

At this point, **Mr. Hand** walks up to Spicoli's desk and takes the pizza away from him and says:

> "You're absolutely right, Mr. Spicoli. It is our time. Yours, mine and everyone else's in this room. But it is my class."

> **Mr. Hand** then picks a few students to come up to the front of the class where he says, "Mr. Spicoli has been kind enough to bring us a snack. Be my guest. Help yourselves. Get a good one."

In less than a minute, the entire pizza is gone, and Spicoli is left with an empty pizza box and an empty stomach.

So the workplace lesson we get from this interaction is:

 When ordering lunch in the office, make sure to get enough for everyone.

Especially when it's pizza, everyone loves a good pizza! In fact, everyone loves a bad pizza. It's pizza, and it's just the best food ever.

CHAPTER 5

THE LOST BOYS

"Come on, be one of us."

David, *The Lost Boys*

Beyond the business lessons of course, if there is one thing that we learned from '80s movies, it's that the underdogs, outcasts and the neo-maxi zoom dweebies can also be the ass-kickers. In one of my favorite supernatural movies of all time, *The Lost Boys*, the vampires are the coolest of the cool and David the leader of the bloodsuckers is cool personified. He's smooth, smart, drives a wicked motorcycle, has fashion sense that's combination rock star and 15th-century pirate, and is portrayed by Kiefer Sutherland (so that alone gives him a bit of an "it" factor). Because of all of that, we can look past the hint of "business in the front, party in the back" '80s mullet. But it's actually two awkward-looking, unassuming, completely opposite of cool, comic-book-store-managing brothers who provide us with our first lesson: **Problem solvers don't come in a one-size-fits-all package.**

I remember the first time in my business career that I decided it was unnecessary to put the time in to review the legalese in a contract. After all, what could it possibly say that we couldn't negotiate our way out of later on, right? Ah, yes acting just like the New Kid on the Block that I was before becoming a Real Genius on all things contractual. In business, like in life, we sometimes have to learn the hard way, and such was the case with this contract. The vendor didn't live up to their side of the contract and the agreed-to timeline for delivery of our merchandise. Unfortunately, they were under no obligation to hit our deadline because the contract stated (in very small print) that they could not guarantee the delivery date of the items unless they had a six-week lead time. We only gave them four weeks, and they were unwilling to eat the costs of the items, which led to my first experience with something called "a lesson learned."

At the beginning of *The Lost Boys*, we meet Michael, the older brother of our main character, Sam, who quickly becomes smitten with a girl — Star — who hangs with what looks like a motorcycle gang. Hint: They are vampires. Michael so desperately wants to be part of the group and be close to her that when the bloodsuckers offer him a drink in a bejeweled goblet/bottle, he quickly consumes it, ignoring the warnings from Star that it is blood. And, of course, as most of us know from our real-life experiences with vampires, drinking blood will turn you into one of them. As Michael sees signs of turning into a full-time bloodsucker, his situation reminds us that we should: **Always review the terms and conditions and always read the fine print.**

So, before we go vampire hunting in the workplace, let's travel back in time *Flight-of-the-Navigator* style to July 1987.

That July, I was looking for the magical 17-year-old guy "look how cool I am" elixir that would propel me through the remainder of my last high school summer break. Unfortunately, my decision-making skills at the time were similar to every person in an '80s slasher movie who hears a sound in the room with no lights on when they know a killer is on the loose and then goes to investigate anyway while asking "Is anyone there? Hello?" Very bad decision-making skills. So bad, in fact, I ultimately cut lines in my hair and colored them with green and yellow permanent magic marker. That, combined with neon bright Jams shirts and those skinnier-than-skinny parachute pants, made for a delicious fashion combination. Yup. Magical elixir indeed.

This was also the summer when I attempted to perfect the *Dukes of Hazzard* car jump using my hand-me-down, cherry red, 1977 Delta 88 Oldsmobile, known by my friends as The Beast.

The railroad tracks at the bottom of the hill sat on what looked like a uniquely oversized speedbump, which in our minds translated to one thing ... a ramp. Yes, the combined intellect of six 17-year-old boys is matched only by their proclivity for really stupid ideas. Off we went racing down the hill in The Beast toward a "ramp" and what we could only assume was a primo spot in the annals of *Awesome Moments in Franklin High School History*. Now if we just had a flux capacitor, oh the places we could have gone, but alas, we could only hit 79 mph, which was more than enough to send us airborne. We were halfway down the hill, and my friends were yelling "Faster! Faster!" and all I had running through my head was the current Top 20 hit "Point of No Return" by Expose. As we hit the bottom of the ramp and The Beast started to ascend, the courageous yelling to "Go faster!" turned into an eerie silence that made it seem as if everything was in slow motion. I do recall my hands gripping the steering wheel tighter and a lack of oxygen as I opened my mouth to scream, only to deliver a high-pitched back-of-the-throat whistling sound. Then, with a thud, we were on land again as The Beast pitched back and forth before finally coming to a stop in a ditch off the right side of the road roughly 20 feet from the railroad tracks.

 FUN FACT: The railroad track scene in the classic 1986 movie *Stand by Me* (shameless plug — it is also in book #1) where the boys dodge the train was filmed with a telephoto lens that made the train look like it was right behind them when, actually, it was at the complete opposite end of the tracks.

Now, I don't know much about cars, but I was pretty sure that the sounds we heard coming from under the hood, and the fact that the front passenger door was touching the ground, were not good signs. As the shock of flying through the air wore off, everyone looked at each other with a mix of relief and terror. And once it was clear that all of us were okay, there was a sudden eruption of cheers and laughter followed by a collective "Let's do it again!"

I should add that when I said, "flying through the air," looking back, we couldn't have been more than six inches off the ground, but as far as our classmates were concerned, it was no less than 10 feet.

The summer of '87 provided us with some incredible music for creating some very high-quality mixtapes for the Walkman or the poolside boombox. Once again, there was something for everyone, and this is one of the reasons that the '80s was such an incredible decade. "La Bamba" by Los Lobos was doing a great job teaching the masses a bit of Spanish while U2's, "I Still Haven't Found What I'm Looking For" was sitting at #2 on the charts but #1 in songs sung in your car with the windows rolled up. Speaking of #1, "Shakedown" by Bob Seger (from the movie *Beverly Hills Cop 2*) had the top spot, and Suzanne Vega was adding an important societal message to the billboard charts with "Luka," a song about child abuse.

FUN FACT: After The Artist Formerly Known as Prince, who had already achieved mega-star status, heard the song "Luka," he penned a short, handwritten note to Suzanne Vega to let her know how beautiful the song was and the impact that it had on him when he listened to it. It's a short poetic note, and his penmanship is just as magical as his music. Suzanne Vega shared it with the world when she posted it on social media after he passed away suddenly.

On TV, we were introduced to a series of short animated segments named "The Simpsons" on *The Tracey Ullman Show*, which debuted on the new Fox TV Network along with *Married with Children*. This was the first time since 1955 that primetime television in the US had four networks. We were enjoying the debut season of the incredibly popular *Unsolved Mysteries*, which provided us with the earliest indications that a 24-hour channel about murder mysteries could be a real thing one day. And, well, we now have Discovery ID. *Candid Camera* was providing us with weekly hijinks, and we'd recently said goodbye to the show *Fame*, but the song will live forever.

At the box office, part IV was not a lucky number as *Superman IV: Quest for Peace* and *Jaws IV: The Revenge* were crashing to earth and drowning in knee-deep water respectively. On the positive side, we were being introduced to the late, great R. Lee Ermey as the drill sergeant in the classic *Full Metal Jacket* and having some fun again with "Achmel ... Achwell ...," Axel Foley in *Beverly Hills Cop 2*. One of the most underrated '80s comedies in this guy's humble opinion, *Summer School* was giving us one last laugh before real school started again and James Bond, Timothy Dalton-style premiered at #1 with *The Living Daylights*.

But it was the movie that premiered this week at #2 that gives us our lessons for this chapter. *The Lost Boys* — directed by Joel Schumacher and starring Kiefer Sutherland, Jason Patric, Jami Gertz, Corey Haim and Corey Feldman — entered the halls of movie cult stardom debuting on July 31, 1987. It tells the story of two brothers — Michael and Sam — who move with their divorced mom to Santa Carla, California, and move in with their grandfather. They are drawn to the boardwalk, where they start spending the vast majority of their time and where Sam meets The Frog Brothers — Edgar and Alan — who run a comic book store and will be the focal point for one of our lessons. After an awkward interview of sorts, they inform Sam that their side job is vampire hunting and that Santa Carla is infested with them. As Edgar says of their comic book store job, "This is just a cover; we're dedicated to a higher purpose. We're fighters for truth, justice, and the American way."

Meanwhile Michael — the older of the two brothers — has met a girl on the boardwalk whose name is Star and is promptly visited by David (played by Kiefer Sutherland) and his crew who look more like a motorcycle gang than a gaggle of vampires. (Not sure what you would call a group of vampires, and I like the word gaggle, so gaggle it is!) Michael wants to fit in and be part of the group so he drinks from a bottle that is offered to him even though Star warns him that it is actually blood and that he should not drink it. And just like that, Michael is, as David says, "one of us" — well, he's halfway to vampire status.

As the movie progresses, Sam begins to piece things together and realizes that his older brother is going through a "transformation" of sorts. Once the vampire-hunting Frog Brothers catch wind of this, they tell Sam that he will need to stake his brother through the heart, which is clearly not an option for Sam. When Michael realizes that he is getting closer to full-time vampire status, he asks for help and leads Sam and The Frog Brothers to the vampire lair during the day to take care of the infestation once and for all. Things don't go exactly as planned, but ultimately, they rid Santa Carla of all things vampire and, thanks to The Frog Brothers, their little idyllic beach town is safe once again.

So what did our awkward but courageous Frog Brothers and our gaggle of vampires teach us about today's workplace?

Problem solvers don't come in a one-size-fits-all package

When we meet The Frog Brothers — Alan and Edgar — they don't exactly inspire comparisons to the movie badass problem solvers of all-time like Chuck Norris, Bruce Lee or Clint Eastwood. Here we have two teenage boys running their parents' comic book store with a combined fighting weight of 180 pounds dressed in scarves posing as bandanas, styling in the oh-so-popular '80s feathered haircuts and wearing Army surplus store t-shirts. Of course, they talk a big game, especially the first time that Sam wanders into their store and they follow him around until he asks if they have a problem — to which Alan replies, "Just scoping out your civilian wardrobe." Later in the same scene, they hand Sam their business card with a "There's our number on the back. And pray you never need to call us."

It's this attitude and confidence, along with their outer physical appearance, that reminds us of another uniquely suited problem solver from earlier in the decade, Johnny Gasparini, the skinny switchblade comb-toting "I want my two dollars" paperboy from *Better Off Dead*. Persistent and focused, but also with a fighting weight well below anything resembling intimidating, he used body language, facial expressions and tone when attacking a problem — "Four weeks, 20 papers, that's two dollars. Plus tip." When he heard excuses like "Gee Johnny, I don't have a dime," he replies with "Didn't ask for a dime. Two dollars ... cash." We will hear more from him later in this book, so don't peek.

One of the really great lessons for all of us that '80s movies brought en masse to the silver screen for the first time was the idea that you didn't need a cape or insane physical stature or Liam Neeson's "particular set of skills" to be a problem solver. I mean, sure, we had our share of Arnold movies where he singlehandedly destroys an entire country's military and the late great Christopher Reeves who donned the Superman cape on a few occasions throughout the decade. But we also had nerds, geeks, outcasts, loners, quirky basket-cases and brothers named after the most sought-after animal for dissection in high school biology classes of yore ... The Frog Brothers. Prior to the '80s, all of these characters and personalities wouldn't have gotten a second look when it came to creating the very best cinematic problem solvers.

> *One of the really great lessons for all of us that '80s movies brought en masse to the silver screen for the first time was the idea that you didn't need a cape or insane physical stature or Liam Neeson's "particular set of skills" to be a problem solver.*

On the surface, Alan and Edgar Frog would most likely not be your choice to rid your neighborhood or your business of vampires. Yes, all of our businesses have them, too, just not in the literal Anne Rice or Bram Stoker-sense that we know them. These vampires suck the positive out of the room, office or meeting the minute they enter and no amount of garlic or holy water will stop them. Believe me; I've tried. But that is a lesson for another day.

What Alan and Edgar teach us, in all their awkwardness, ridiculousness and misplaced bravado, is that problem solvers don't have a standardized and uniform look. They don't come in a one-size-fits-all package. So, as the Santa Carla boardwalk is plastered with missing persons flyers and the police are attempting to solve the crimes from a traditional perspective, the brothers are taking a different approach ... convinced that the "problem" is not quite as it seems. But honestly, who is going to take them seriously when (in the words of one my favorite poets, Tom Petty) they are claiming that it's actually "all the vampires walkin' through the valley, mov(ing) west down Ventura Boulevard" who are responsible for the spike in disappearances?

Now, let's think about this from a workplace perspective. In the vast majority of businesses, the leaders are looked to when there are problems that need to be solved. It's understandable, of course, in the hierarchal sense, and we've all heard the phrase "That's above my pay grade," which is often muttered by the Buzzword Bob of the office. But do leaders always have the right answers, and will they be able to solve every problem?

If you've ever been a position of leadership, you know there are sometimes influencing factors that contribute to how a problem can be solved. And those influencing factors don't always take you directly to the solution. They are usually unfortunate factors, like corporate politics, budget constraints, resources and, my personal favorite, egos. I've just never understood how so many companies allow egos to get in the way of their success. It's really quite remarkable. There isn't a single redeeming quality you can point to that comes from having Ernie Ego running around your office getting in the way of progress, but every business has one, and the bigger a business gets, the more they multiply. Kind of like Gremlins but without the need for water, sunlight or post-midnight feedings.

> *There isn't a single redeeming quality you can point to that comes from having Ernie Ego running around your office getting in the way of progress, but every business has one, and the bigger a business gets, the more they multiply.*

So, do leaders always have the right answers, and can they solve every problem? No, they don't — not even close — and if you are a leader and you believe that you do, then you aren't a true leader. You are more of an Ernie Ego. With all of the issues that most companies are dealing with on a daily basis, your true problem solvers are probably being overlooked and not considered for a seat at the "adult" table (that's tongue in cheek, by the way). When I worked for a company that shall remain unnamed, we had been trying to solve a problem that was having a major negative influence on our cost per lead. We looked for the solution in marketing and then extended our net to include sales and accounting. All of the so-called big guns decided that the best thing we could do was set up a weekly conference call to continue discussing ideas and try to find a solution. I usually hate this idea, but I was early in my career and hadn't quite found the *Freddie Mercury* in my corporate voice. Well, thankfully, so did our chief marketing officer as she felt that enough time and money had been spent on problem-solving the traditional way. Because we weren't getting any real solutions from the Ernie and Ellen Egos of the leadership team, it was time to try something different. And different she tried. Like *Edward Scissorhands* different. She showed the strength and confidence that we learned about in our last chapter through the "I don't know" lesson and posted what amounted to a "help wanted" sign in each break area on every floor of the building. And she didn't ask people to email their ideas to some random "knowledge" or "ideas" box. Nope. She asked them to present their idea/answer at a roundtable that was set for the following week, and she made two things clear:

1. There was no need for a formal presentation. She didn't want people spending time putting together the dreaded PowerPoint deck. Just come in and tell us how you would solve the problem.

2. This was open to everyone. And not just the employees of the business who worked in a cube or office. Literally anyone. The overnight cleaning crew, the delivery person, the guy who filled the vending machines in the break-room. Anyone.

Then she made one thing very clear to the management team — our fearless leaders. Leave your ego and your title at the door. If you couldn't do that, then you were not welcome. Period.

So the day arrived, and all of us were as curious as those red hats that *Devo* wore. Who would show up? Would anyone? Well, yes, yes they did — in droves and quite honestly, we didn't recognize all of them, but here they were, our team members mixed with a few people in work uniforms, all waiting patiently to present their idea to solve the problem. It was awesome. A truly diverse set of individuals — some dressed up, some dressed down, some with name patches on their chest and even one gentleman in a tuxedo. The kicker for me — the real eye-opener — was that not one of them looked like our perceived and naïve definition of a problem-solver in the corporate sense. None of them could have been mistaken for someone sitting on the other side of the door waiting to judge them, and I think deep down we all knew that one or more were going to be the problem-solvers she was hoping to find when she brainstormed this little experiment.

We watched as the march of overlooked Frog Brothers and Frog Sisters walked into the conference room, and the eclectic nature of the group reminded me of the Dear Mr. Vernon letter in *The Breakfast Club* — "...a princess and a basket case, an athlete, a criminal and a brain." In a word, it was cool. After all was said and done, not only did we solve our little problem but we also uncovered several new problem solvers, two of whom became members of the marketing team (one an intern and the other an admin attending night school), one who was promoted within her own department and one who was so impressive that she became the head of a new cross-departmental team created to tackle issues that impacted multiple areas of the business. She was potentially the most "Frog Brother/Sister" of them all. Why? Because for five years she sat in a non-descript cube in a non-descript area of the office analyzing spreadsheets for two of our products along with 10 other people while being overlooked for any true problem-solving opportunities. She was sitting right there in the office for five years with all of this incredible ability but overlooked because she didn't look the part. And I don't mean the fashion or physical sense, like The Frog Brothers, although unfortunately even in 2019 many offices still struggle with those types of issues. What I mean is that she was unassuming in her role because it only required connecting basic data points to each other and, like working in your parents' comic book store, it wasn't a position that screamed "superhero problem solver."

But that's exactly what she was, and just like our protagonists for this chapter, she reminded all of us that problem solvers do not come in a one-size-fits-all package. So, the next time you need to rid the office of a nasty vampire infestation, or you have a more modern-day problem like how to rid the office of a nasty positivity-sucking infestation or find a solution to an unending problem in the business, don't be afraid to post a "help wanted" sign. You may be surprised by who actually has the best solution, and at the very least you will create an atmosphere of inclusion, which is the modern-day garlic and holy water to Ernie and Ellen Ego. Of course, there's the more straightforward approach to Ernie and Ellen Ego — a stake through the heart — but it could be misconstrued as a little uncivilized in the modern workplace.

★ Always review the terms and conditions and always read the fine print

As I mentioned earlier in the chapter, when David, the vampire leader, says to Michael, "Drink some of this, Michael. Be one of us," he is handing him a glass of blood that will expedite his transition to a creature of the night. Well, more like a goblet-bottle kind of thing but for this lesson, it's more about what's in the container than the container itself. Whether Michael is aware that it is actually blood, colored water or some drug-infused concoction is never really clear because it would seem that he has no idea that this clean-cut (sarcasm) crew of misfits are actually vampires. He is the new kid in town and desperately trying to impress Star, who is also part of this new group and with whom he quickly becomes smitten when he sees her on the boardwalk for the first time.

Star is well aware that Michael is about to embark on a very dangerous and uncertain journey and, while the rest of the crew is imploring him to drink, she says, "Don't. You don't have to, Michael ... it's blood." But Michael, because of either bravado, naïveté or misplaced trust, says "Yeah, right," and drinks from the goblet-bottle thing. Let's just say that things trend downward from there for Michael. He finds himself trapped in an unforgiving and one-sided contract that teaches him a chaotic, terrifying and painful lesson in the consequences of not reviewing the fine print.

He finds himself trapped in an unforgiving and one-sided contract that teaches him a chaotic, terrifying and painful lesson in the consequences of not reviewing the fine print.

Eventually, Michael finds himself transforming — difficulties with daylight, a fear of crosses and garlic, and the disappearance of his reflection in the mirror — which prompts his younger brother Sam to go on a rant about his older brother being a vampire, which ends with him saying, "You wait til Mom finds out." Oh, how many times I heard that from my younger sister growing up. I always felt like the villain in the *Scooby-Doo* cartoon saying, "I would have gotten away with it if it wasn't for my meddling sister." But once again, I digress.

When Michael foolishly waves off the advice of his counsel
(Star) and goes forward with drinking from the goblet-bottle
thing, he, in some ways, represents where many of us have been
when it comes to analyzing the fine print and reading the terms
and conditions of a business contract. Forgive us for our lack of
enthusiasm in our commitment to read through the mountains
of legalese that would be best described, in the words of Phil
Collins, as a "Land of Confusion." In most of these situations,
we were likely our own counsel launching our own product,
starting our own company or even cutting corners to deliver
a project that, as usual, has an unrealistic timeframe.

Oftentimes, our lack of attention to these details is due to the
fact that, like Michael, we are excited about the potential for
a new opportunity. Maybe it's your first big contract for your
new business, and you've worked so hard to get to this point
that you just want to close the deal and (in the words of Kool
and the Gang) "Celebrate good times." Or maybe you are new to
a position and under pressure on a large project and don't feel
as if you have the time to review the terms and conditions from
the vendor that is going to help you hit a rapidly approaching
deadline. It could be that you've been working around the clock
on your side hustle and you finally have someone interested in
the product or service that you've been building at night and
on weekends while foregoing any semblance of a social life.
Hmmm ... now that sounds incredibly familiar to this author.
But, as Michael found out, when those pesky little terms and
conditions are overlooked, they are capable of delivering
a full-on Ivan Drago uppercut that can leave you flat on your
back, unable to fight back on your own.

I've seen this first-hand both in contracts and proofreading, which is also a form of "fine print," particularly to those of us who are marketers. The first example was a contract that I inherited at the beginning of a new job, which involved a new opportunity for the company that leadership was very excited about and keen to get started. So much so that the excitement to implement this new initiative blinded some incredibly smart people to the obvious pitfalls within the contract they were signing.

FUN FACT: Pitfall, a video game released by Activision, was the best-selling home video game of 1982 and sold more than 4 million copies on the Atari 2600 platform. The broadcast commercial for the game featured a 13-year-old Jack Black.

The contract called for the creation of six programs within a 7-month period with much of the content and creative work falling on our team. This was fine, and expected, as the vendor was providing the platform and all the services for each program. However, in the rush of excitement to bring one of these programs to market, there were two major problems within the contract that were overlooked:

1. **Timing** — We had a very small team responsible for all aspects of global marketing and communications, so implementing a new project with multiple touchpoints under a tight timeline was a bit like "hitting the connecting

wire at 88 mph the instant the lightning struck the tower."
In a word, difficult. In this case — if created from scratch,
which was our situation — each one of the six programs
would typically have an implementation timeline of
90 days. This was the agreed-to industry standard, and
anything less would run the risk of a very low success rate
or outright failure. So, let's go back to our terms and conditions — six programs within a 7-month period. Now, no
one is going to mistake my intellectual prowess for Lewis,
Gilbert or Wormser from *Revenge of the Nerds* but even with
my limited numeric skills, I can come to the conclusion that
the math doesn't work. Best-case scenario would have been
that we delivered two programs in the contracted timeframe. We didn't.

2. **Flexibility** — The contract was written in such a way that
    the onus was on us — the customer — to deliver. From
    the vendor's point of view, as well as the language in
    the contract, there was zero flexibility in the number of
    programs and the timeframe afforded to use their services
    to deliver on said programs. Actually, the wording in the
    contract made it more like *Less Than Zero* flexibility minus
    appearances from Robert Downey, Jr., James Spader and
    Jami Gertz, which would have made the pill a little less diffi-
    cult to swallow.

And here was the kicker — the $15,500 that our company paid
for their services for the six programs was required upfront in
full and was non-refundable, regardless of the amount of work
actually done. Because the fees were for services including
consulting and customer operations and not for manufac-
tured products that would sit in inventory, it would stand to

reason that we should be able to use those hours at any time. But those pesky terms and conditions that went unread clearly stated that all support hours must be used within the 7-month timeframe and that no hours or services could be rolled over. In other words, because our representatives drank from the goblet-bottle thing without analyzing what was actually inside, we paid $15,500 for one program rather than the standard $2,580 for each of six. Not ideal. Coming in late, I did all I could to re-negotiate but even channeling the sales skills of both Joel Goodson (Tom Cruise) from *Risky Business* and Billy Ray Valentine (Eddie Murphy) from *Trading Places* didn't allow me to overcome the realities of the "fine print."

Our second story comes from the marketing world but is an example for anyone in business who may consider putting expediency over evaluation, much as our friend Michael did. This one can definitely fit in the category of reading the fine print and rereading it and then reviewing it.

Years ago, in the time of knights and dragons, I worked for a full-service ad agency. We had a very good run for a few years. It was fun, exciting work and most importantly, there was an endless variety of clients ranging from high fashion to transportation software. Personally, I do my best work when I can jump from project to project without having to immerse myself for hours on end in one project unless, of course, it is writing books on '80s pop culture and what it teaches us about today's workplace.

One beautiful South Florida afternoon, we had a potential client walk through our doors with a very interesting story. He was the marketing director for a pharmaceutical company and told us that he had spent the past month doing research on local ad agencies, so it seemed as if he was someone who believed in due diligence. At the very least, it would seem that he did his homework before making decisions or moving forward with a partnership or project.

We showed him around the agency and did our standard "dog and pony show." For those who are not familiar with the term, it's basically what agencies and sometimes project managers call their pitch to prospects. In terms of '80s movie analogies, think of it like the volleyball scene from *Top Gun,* where you go a little over the top to show off your best skills in your best package in the very best of environments.

FUN FACT: *Over the Top* was a 1987 film starring (and co-written by) Sylvester Stallone. It tells the story of a truck driver who arm wrestles on the side and uses this skill in an attempt to win tournaments that will assist him in reuniting with the son he hasn't seen in 10 years. Critics panned it, but I actually like it, if for nothing more than the soundtrack and the fact that Stallone turns his hat backward before each arm-wrestling match as if it is some kind of superhero cape that he throws over his shoulders.

After our presentation, this client began to tell us why he was looking for an agency to assist with his marketing programs moving forward, and it was a doozy. As a way to market a new drug to doctors' offices, they had decided to provide their outside sales team with different flavored popcorn in branded bags with the pharma company's name, the drug name, website address, email and phone number. It was the last one — the phone number — that ultimately made him *Walk This Way* — in the words of Run DMC and Aerosmith and in the literal sense — into our little ad agency.

But let's quickly go back to Michael and his overzealousness to drink from the goblet-bottle thing. Two of the reasons that he decided to handle it the way that he did were (a) to impress a new group and (b) to expedite his acceptance by the group. There were a number of other reasons (some of which we've mentioned), but it is because of these two that our soon-to-be-new client found himself in quite a pickle. He had only been with the company for a few months and was tasked with finding a way to promote a new drug on a mass scale quickly and in a budget-friendly manner. For those of us in marketing, this is no easy task, but it's one that we have all been faced with on multiple occasions. Our soon-to-be new client was, shall we say, a little fresh-faced and in his first real marketing ownership/leadership role so, of course, impressing the leadership team quickly was one of his main goals. This project would give him his chance.

Unfortunately, it didn't go as planned, and in his desire to please so quickly, he failed to do something that, since then, I've made part of every project checklist I've written. That task is very simple but often an afterthought due to its simplicity — check the phone number and then check it again and then call it to make sure it's right. Yes, in his quest for immediate acceptance, he expedited the printing and proofreading process by assuming the phone number was correct on 400,000 popcorn bags that were all delivered to doctors' offices over the course of several days. It wasn't until the end of the week when the first call came in from one of their pharmaceutical sales reps (and then another and another until there were more phone calls from the sales team than there were from their target audience — the doctors' offices) that it became clear, to use an '80s word, just how — gnarly — it was.

The phone number was off by one digit — just one digit — and the results were horrifying for him and honestly, humorous for us (of course, after he was gone). Rather than doctors calling a number to get information on the new drug, they instead ended up calling what we will rebrand for this book as an "adult conversation and chat line designed for intimate talk." Everyone in the company — from the doctors to the outside salespeople to the marketing director and probably the "operators" on the other end — got a little more than they expected and not in a good way. All because the need to quickly please outweighed the reading of the fine print, or in this instance, the simple check of a phone number. Of course, if the number was mistakenly printed as 867-5309, in an homage to the '80s one-hit musical wonder Tommy Tutone, it may have made for a better story (at least in my eyes).

Ultimately, the client did point the finger at both the printer and the agency, blaming each of them for this unfortunate turn of events, which as I think about it could prompt another lesson about the importance of taking responsibility and being accountable to your job and your actions. Because we did realize there was the potential for us to be his next scapegoat should something go wrong, we carefully and meticulously reviewed the terms and conditions in our contract with him and his company as well as the fine print before we agreed to work with him. And then, of course, we read the terms and conditions again.

So, if you find yourself in Michael's position — minus of course the goblet bottle-thing with an unidentified liquid — excited to impress at a new job, eager to finalize a new opportunity or seeing the potential for your side hustle to turn into something real, just remember that the terms and conditions and fine print are written to be read. And read again. After all, you don't want to rely on a sibling or a friend to keep you from being staked in the heart by two crazy vampire-hunting brothers named after an amphibian. Trust me on this one.

Remember that the terms and conditions and fine print are written to be read. And read again.

CHAPTER 6

COMING TO AMERICA

"When you think of garbage, think of Akeem."

Prince Akeem, *Coming to America*

I'll bet you are wondering to yourself, *"Of all the great quotes in* Coming to America, *why would Chris pick that one to open this chapter?"* Great question! Yes, I absolutely recognize that, between the guys in the barbershop and the vocally challenged Randy Watson, there's a treasure trove of classic quotes from this movie — some of which we may get to enjoy later in this chapter. But when we think of lessons for the workplace from this movie, we start with Eddie Murphy's character, Prince Akeem, and a valuable lesson in: **How unearned leadership creates pleasers while earned leadership creates believers.**

After all, if someone of royal blood is proud to take out the trash, they can certainly teach us about the right way to lead.

And in leaving the comforts of a royal family in the fictional African country of Zamunda for the less comfy confines of Queens, NY, our lovable Prince Akeem also teaches us how: **Putting ourselves in unfamiliar territory can do wonders for our career growth.**

In actuality, *Coming to America* is workplace-lesson gold and choosing just two lessons was as challenging as deciding whether to use my last two quarters on Space Ace or Dragon's Lair at the Space Station Arcade in my local mall back in 1983.

Okay, let's hop in our Delorean once again, and travel back in time to June of 1988, when *Coming to America* hit the box office, and set the scene for our workplace lessons.

Ah, yes, June of 1988. I had just graduated from high school, and my terrible, awful, no-good senior prom song was still stuck in my head. That song? "I've Had the Time of My Life" from *Dirty Dancing,* whose only saving grace was the fact that it starred the magical Patrick Swayze. Those of you who read my first book know how much of a man-crush I have on that guy — very large — but he is also responsible for providing the outlet that prompted our senior class to overwhelmingly vote for that horrific song as our prom theme. I mean one of the hottest songs at the time was "Nothin' But a Good Time" from those '80s glam rockers, Poison, which would have been the perfect choice, but it didn't stand a chance against Johnny and Baby's romantic tome.

Bad prom songs aside, I was preparing for my freshman year of college by heading down to Ocean City, Maryland, to live for the summer with seven other guys in a 3-bedroom house.

The ratio of bedrooms to humans wasn't great, but we did have an amazing summer, and I secured a job at Candy Kitchen, shoveling fudge and gummy rats to tourists each and every day. Besides a very unwise decision to fry and eat eggs that had been left out for several days (in a pan that hadn't been washed in several weeks), I made it through fairly unscathed — well at least as far as you will know for now.

Summers in the '80s always provided an awesome mix of popular music for laying out at the beach with Sun-In and lemon juice on many a head of blonde (or would-be blonde) hair, including mine. And once again the Top 40 was showing its incredibly eclectic nature. How eclectic, you ask? Well consider this — The Church, with their alternative style and melodic tones in their song "Under the Milky Way," was sitting at #26 bookended by hall-of-famer Robert Plant's "Tall Cool One" and pin-up-girl-turned-musician *Samantha Fox* and her catchy dance hit, "Naughty Girls Need Love Too." Throw in some Michael Jackson with his millionth hit of the decade, "Dirty Diana," and one of the all-time great rock bands, Def Leppard, with "Pour Some Sugar on Me," and you've got yourself musical Top 40 diversity. And that is without mentioning J.J. Fad's "Supersonic" and the man who inspired the Rick-Rolled phenomenon and thousands of memes, Rick Astley with "Together Forever."

Summertime in the '80s was typically a very slow season for any type of momentous television moment. However, we were just a month removed from saying a two-hour goodbye to my favorite, *Magnum P.I.*, whose reruns give me the feeling of putting on my most comfortable pair of jeans. We had also recently said goodbye to *St. Elsewhere*, which starred Howie

Mandel, who I idolized so much as a comedian that I did an impersonation of his character Bobby for my senior high school talent show. And we were just two weeks away from the first edition of *Shark Week,* which 30 years later is still keeping people out of the water, while sports fans like myself were just a little over a month away from the first official night game at Wrigley Field, which was televised as a prime time edition of the Game of the Week.

The price of movies was rising rapidly, and it was becoming more difficult to find a ticket under $3.00, but that didn't stop the masses from making the pilgrimage to local theatres. The box office wasn't lacking for star power with Tom Hanks, Kevin Costner, Sylvester Stallone, Dan Aykroyd, John Candy and John Hughes all represented at the top. *Big* was "shimmy shimmy cocoa popping" its way to #3 while *Bull Durham* was providing laughs to a more "mature" audience. John Rambo was doing Rambo things in *Rambo III* and *The Great Outdoors* was showing, once again, that comedy with a heart sells.

But it was the movie premiering at number one this week that is the basis for our lessons in this chapter. *Coming to America* starring Eddie Murphy, Arsenio Hall and James Earl Jones, and directed by John Landis (who also directed arguably the most famous music video in history — Thriller), hit theatres on June 28, 1988.

FUN FACT: Two soon-to-be famous and fantastic actors — Samuel L. Jackson and Cuba Gooding, Jr. — both had small bit parts in *Coming to America*. Jackson played "hold up man" while

Gooding, Jr., played "boy getting haircut." Safe to
say that both went on to have just a slight bit
of success.

~~~~~~

The movie tells the story of Prince Akeem Joffer (played by
Eddie Murphy) from the fictional African country of Zamunda
and his quest to find the love of his life. Based on his station in
life as royalty, his parents arrange a marriage for him at the age
of 21. But the prince is not interested in this lifestyle and wants
to both prove he can survive on his own and find a woman who
will love him for who he is and not for his title and fortune. He
grabs his assistant Semmi (played by Arsenio Hall), and they
head for America. More specifically Queens, NY, because as
Semmi asks, "But where in New York can one find a woman
with grace and elegance? A woman suitable for a King?" to
which Akeem says, "Queens!" And with that, they are off.

Through a local community event, Akeem meets and quickly
falls for Lisa McDowell, but she has a boyfriend Daryl, whose
father owns Soul Glo, a very successful hairstyling aid company.
Lisa's father Cleo owns fast-food restaurant McDowell's
("home of the Big Mick"), which is a not-so-subtle rip-off of
McDonald's all the way down to the golden arches. Although
Daryl is annoying, spoiled and obnoxious, Lisa's father
believes that he is the best person for her because his family
is successful as well and this seems to be the most important
thing to him.

Akeem and Semmi take entry-level jobs at McDowell's to
learn the values of hard work and, of course, so Akeem can get
closer to Lisa. Akeem embraces all aspects of the work while

Semmi struggles to get comfortable outside of the royal palace. Eventually, Akeem begins dating Lisa, much to the chagrin of her father (you see, Akeem has told everyone that he was a poor goat herder back in his country). King Jaffe (James Earl Jones), Akeem's father, comes to Queens to bring him back to Zamunda where he can live the life that has been bestowed upon him, but Akeem loves Lisa. She is upset that Akeem lied to her and does not want to see him anymore, so he goes back to Zamunda as requested and back to his arranged marriage. The movie doesn't end there, but for those who have not seen it, I'll refrain from being the spoiler. Honestly, if you haven't seen it, stop reading right now and go watch it. You can come back later. The words will still be here on the page. I promise.

So, what did our humble Prince Akeem teach us about today's workplace?

 Unearned leadership creates pleasers. Earned leadership creates believers.

Oftentimes, how we define leadership is based on our own experiences with a variety of "leaders" we have met throughout our careers and personal lives. Do a Google search on leadership, and it won't take long to find thousands of definitions from thousands of people about what makes a great leader. Depending on the industry or background, the definition of great can be different as well. For example, a great military leader might need to show decisiveness, courage, loyalty and organization while a great philanthropic leader might show compassion, openness, altruism and an understanding of business principles. Additionally, a military leader who has spent time in combat or in theater (defined by Merriam-Webster as the entire land, sea and air area that is or may become involved directly in war operations) and the philanthropic leader who spends real time with the people impacted by the very problem they are trying to solve rather than only glad-handing at events, will quickly find real respect from those they lead. Earned leadership.

Near the beginning of the movie, Akeem and his soon-to-be bride are having a conversation in an attempt to get to know each other a little better. The conversation goes like this:

Prince Akeem: "What do you like to do?"

Imani: "Whatever you like."

Prince Akeem: "What kind of music do you like?"

Imani: "Whatever kind of music you like."

Prince Akeem: "What is your favorite food?"

Imani: "Whatever food you like."

Even Semmi, his best and only friend and personal assistant, will ultimately follow Akeem's lead and only question him if he feels that a decision could harm or negatively impact Akeem. And then we have Lisa's dad, Cleo, who does a complete 180 on his view of Akeem as soon as he finds out he is royalty. He showed zero respect to him when he was just an entry-level employee from a poor goat-herding family as revealed in this exchange:

Cleo: "You know how to mop, don't you?"

Akeem: "Oh, yes."

Cleo: "Don't use the bucket. It'll just confuse you."

However, once it is clear that Akeem is Prince Akeem, he says, "A prince. He's a prince. Oh, Lisa, you did it this time. You hit the jackpot. Your little goat herder makes Daryl look like a welfare case." When Cleo meets Akeem's mom, the Queen, he says, "I don't know whether to shake your hand or kiss it or bow or what. I feel like breakdancing."

As a 21-year-old prince who was born into wealth and power, Akeem hasn't proven himself on any kind of leadership level, yet he still has followers. Converts are easy to come by once they know his social status. They don't need to know if he has any real accomplishments or even goals, and the fact that everything he owns or enjoys was given to him without any effort on his part does not matter. Whether it's fear, laziness or a desire to climb socially via a shortcut, his followers are not following out of any kind of true respect. Unearned leadership.

> *Whether it's fear, laziness or a desire to climb socially via a shortcut, his followers are not following out of any kind of true respect. Unearned leadership.*

Let's look at earned leadership versus unearned leadership in a different scenario that I think most of us can relate to. At some point in our lives, most of us have been given something material that we really wanted — usually when we were kids and begged our parents for something until they gave in. You know you were guilty of this at some point, I mean everyone had their figurative Red Rider BB-Gun from the classic holiday movie, *A Christmas Story*. If you are a connoisseur of that movie, then you will also recall the "pink nightmare" moment which some of us (me) actually lived through in reality — but because that has nothing to do with our leadership lesson here, I'll quickly move on before telling you too much more about my awkward childhood.

So, my figurative Red Rider BB-Gun was something called an Omnibot, which I got as a Christmas gift back in my early teens. The Omnibot was a robot that you could program to do basic tasks like deliver food to a room on its tray, carry books or, in the words of the '80s music icon Lionel Ritchie, you could program it to go "Dancing on the Ceiling" to your favorite music. Well actually on the floor but you get the idea. You could even program it to say things like "Hello, my name is Luka," "I'll be back" and "feed me, Seymour." Every time the commercial came on, I made sure to turn up the volume and call my mom into the living room so she could see it. I begged and pleaded for my Omnibot. I even came up with some cockamamie (yes, you don't have to be 93 years old to use that word) idea that it could be programmed to provide educational content. Lo and behold, I arose Christmas morning to find my very own Omnibot under the tree, and a love affair with my toy blossomed ... for three whole weeks, at which point it was relegated to a corner of my bedroom and was eventually laid to rest in the back of my closet. He didn't do anything wrong. I mean this wasn't my mogwai "Don't feed them after midnight" moment from *Gremlins*.

Like Akeem's leadership, my Omnibot was unearned, and because of that, I cared less about the time, effort and cost invested in providing me with this gift. Thankfully, it was clear that based on his actions, Akeem knew his leadership

was unearned as he showed in this exchange with his
father, the King:

> **King Jaffe Joffer**: "And who are you?"

> **Prince Akeem**: "I am a man who has never tied his
> own shoes before!"

> **King Jaffe Joffer**: "Wrong. You are a prince who has never
> tied his own shoes. Believe me. I tied my own shoes once. It
> is an overrated experience."

Akeem desperately tries to get his arranged bride-to-be to
tell him about the things that she enjoys; he encourages his
personal assistant/best friend to challenge him; when he
finds an apartment building in Queens, he purposely asks
for the worst apartment; and he takes a job as an entry-level
employee at a fast food joint so he can learn the value of
a hard day's work. He even takes on garbage duties proudly as
he states, "I have recently been placed in charge of garbage.
Do you have any that requires disposal? When you think of
garbage, think of Akeem."

But in the real world, those who are given their mantle of
leadership unearned are often severely lacking in any type of
humility. On the contrary, they tend to lean more toward an
entitled mentality, that somehow because of their status or
connection to someone in a power position that they deserve
to be a leader. Let me guess — most of you have a wry smile
as you read this and recall someone in your professional life
who resembles this character very closely. They are hard to
forget, and I've had several. Just like my lack of appreciation
for the time, effort and cost that went into my Omnibot, those

in unearned leadership positions tend to lack appreciation or understanding for key leadership qualities, like accountability, empowerment, inspiration and integrity. Rather than earn respect, they demand it, and eventually they drive out the very best that a company, division or team have to offer leaving them with only the pleasers. But pleasers do a very good job pleasing, and that is what the unearned leader seeks.

> *But in the real world, those who are given their mantle of leadership unearned are often severely lacking in any type of humility.*

Fast forward to the following year, and I had my eye on a super sweet dual cassette deck boombox complete with bass boosters. With that in tow, I would be king cat daddy indeed. Of course, there was one small problem — it was $250 — and well, I just spent my last two dollars trying to reclaim the high score on Galaga at my local arcade. What can I say, I needed to see my gamer initials ACE at the top of the leaderboard. But I really wanted that boombox and I took the Omnibot approach, which failed miserably this time around. Thankfully, I did have an option — get a job, and get a job I did. I was officially part of the workforce, making $2.25 an hour as a dishwasher in a local restaurant, and it was magnificent. Yeah, my mom had to drive me and pick me up, which she gladly did.

There I was, cleaner of plates and pots and beverage glasses along with one of my good friends from school. Even though we were being paid less than minimum wage, it was still a fun environment for my first real job. We had the occasional late-night food fight after the rest of the staff had left, and sometimes the chef would let us try some of the artsy dishes they created (although my guess is that we looked like Josh [Tom Hanks] in the movie *Big* when he attempted unsuccessfully to eat caviar and treated baby corn as if it was on the cob). Throughout it all, I had my boombox goal, and when I achieved it, I also appreciated it. So much so that it went to college with me four and a half years later. I earned it and so unlike my Ominbot; I understood the time, effort and cost that went into making it happen. This is also true of earned leadership, and it's why leaders who earn their position value things like responsibility, motivation, positivity and commitment. Rather than demand respect, they earn it, which creates believers. In the corporate sense, when people believe in someone, they do what's necessary for the business, their team and their leader to succeed. Earned leadership creates believers.

Earned leadership creates believers.

In '80s terms, if unearned leadership can be represented by every guy in a romantic comedy who wore a sweater tied around his neck, then earned leadership is the "kickboxing sport of the future" coolness that is Lloyd Dobler from *Say Anything*. Be like Lloyd.

 Putting ourselves in unfamiliar territory can do wonders for our career growth.

When Akeem decided to venture out from the safety of Zamunda and leave behind a royal life full of pampering and riches for the rough and tumble confines of Queens, NY, he could not have picked a location more opposite of his homeland. There's a line in Paula Abdul's 1989 hit song "Opposites

Attract," "Things in common there just ain't a one," which would sum up the two locales perfectly. The fictional Zamunda is a fantastically wealthy, safe, polite, clean country with a landscape straight out of a Monet painting. Contrast that with Queens, which is portrayed in the film as a downtrodden, crime-ridden, rude, filthy city where even the colors of a rainbow are drab. And before I find my email inbox filled with hate, I should point out that it was Queens 30 years ago and from a fictional movie. Please, please, please let that be enough of a disclaimer. The Queens of today is very different and was the location for one of my favorite sitcoms, *King of Queens,* with two of my favorite actors — Kevin James and Leah Remini.

Now, as mentioned previously in the chapter, Akeem had his reasons for going to Queens, and they were noble. He wants to be his own man, experience real work, be treated as if he was any other person, and hopefully find an independent and intelligent woman who will love him for him and not his royal status.

Off he and Semmi go to a very unfamiliar territory with little knowledge of what to anticipate when they arrive. When they do reach Queens, they quickly realize how different it is from their home country, and while Semmi is fearful, Akeem embraces this wonderful new landscape. He does this to such a degree that when the cab driver asks what part of Queens they want to go to, Akeem responds, "Take us to the most common part" and the cabbie obliges. They pull up in front of a rundown building on a block with buildings full of broken windows, people warming their hands over barrels of fire, a barbershop named "My-T-Sharp" (some of the best comedy you will ever see takes place there) and a neighbor nice enough to throw her garbage out of the window and onto the sidewalk right in front of Akeem.

Cab driver: "This shitty enough for ya?"

Akeem: "Yes, this is perfect!"

 FUN FACT: Eddie Murphy and Arsenio Hall each played multiple characters in *Coming to America*. Besides Prince Akeem, Murphy played Randy Watson, lead singer of the band Sexual Chocolate; Clarence, the owner of the My-T-Sharp barbershop; and Saul, the older Jewish My-T-Sharp barbershop customer. Beyond Semmi, Hall also played Morris the barber, the enigmatic Reverend Brown and a female clubgoer.

All of this takes place while both of them are still dressed in their royal garb complete with incredibly large gold jewelry, full-length fur coats and enough luggage to cover all the Griswold family vacations.

Akeem is determined to learn as much as possible from his time away and immerses himself in this new world. He sheds his royal skin with the cutting of a traditional rat tail of sorts that he has been growing on the back of his head since birth and exchanges his fur coat and gold jewelry for jeans, a baseball hat and a jacket covered in New York tourist-style buttons. When they enter their apartment building for the first time, Akeem tells the landlord, "We seek meager accommodations" and "We require a room that is very poor," and they get it. As mentioned earlier, he also takes a job as an entry-level fast food employee and embraces the role of garbage man.

All of this is to say that whether Akeem realizes it or not, he is setting himself up for major growth and in an expedited manner. In embracing the very worst of what his new surroundings have to offer, he is completely removing himself from any opportunity to find familiarity or comfort in his new place. There's nothing to fall back on that could ultimately create complacency, and his choices have already created an environment that would not allow for any type of growth stagnation. Just requesting and being dropped off in the most common place in Queens is growth in itself.

And grow he does. In his willingness to take a menial job, Akeem learns the value of a hard day's work and comes to understand and appreciate the life of someone of non-royalty — a commoner, if you will. His desire to live in the poorest apartment quickly teaches him humility, and he discovers a newfound appreciation for the luck of the life that he inherited. His interactions with real people who only know him as a poor African goat herder or exchange student gives him a new ability to see when someone likes him for him or for his status. Most importantly, he finds out what he's really made of when he is away from all of the majestic pomp and circumstance of his royal stature in Zamunda. And he likes who he finds.

Growth in our careers is much easier to come by today than it was in the generations that came before us. Gone are the days of working for one company over a 40-year period followed by a retirement party that included a gold watch, cake and room full of employees ready to participate in a hearty golf clap at just the right time. Even the way that we job search today provides us with greater opportunities for growth at an expedited rate. We have thousands of jobs right at our fingertips, and we don't have to wait for the newspaper so we can circle the ones we are interested in while perusing the classifieds. We can take on stretch roles outside of our current position, allowing us to learn a new skill and area. We are much more mobile in the living and transportation sense and have the ability to pursue jobs almost anywhere we choose. We can change careers and start fresh at pretty much any age. We can take time away from our career trajectory and spend six months or a year giving back to something we believe in through a volunteer work sabbatical, for example, and then be applauded for it rather than written off when we come back to a new job search. We can even leave a job without a new one and support ourselves through a robust "gig economy" until we figure out our next chapter.

There are many ways for us to expedite our career growth by putting ourselves in unfamiliar territory, yet very few of us actually do it. I've been guilty of it for sure, but as you read this book, I have just left the corporate world after almost 25 years of servitude to continue pursuing my second career as an author and speaker — a pursuit that will quite possibly be supported in some way from the gig economy. This is most definitely unfamiliar territory for me but even before I took the 1988 George Michael leap of "Faith," I was expediting my career growth in this area by doing things for the first time, like book signings, author conversations and speaking at large business conferences. Two of those three put me in very unfamiliar territory, especially considering that the only autograph I'd ever signed previously was in my classmates' high school yearbooks along with an Oscar Wilde quote under my senior picture that said "I have nothing to declare except my genius." That quote paired with my name might very well be history's first example of fake news.

Keeping this lesson in the family — not a royal one by any stretch, mind you — I am the very proud older brother of my only sister, Ashleigh. She is everything that anyone could ask for in a sibling, and it has been an absolute pleasure to see her grow into an incredibly successful woman. Besides the time when she was four years old and ripped to shreds both my comic book and baseball card collections, which earned her the nickname Little Tornado, I've been her biggest fan. I'm bragging about her now because she is the perfect example of what can happen when you embrace the unfamiliar.

My sister majored in communications and took her first post-college job with one of the large credit card companies as a sales/marketing representative. It was the typical entry-level job that could provide a stepping stone for future growth within the company or the industry. Now, our family has always had a deep connection with and a love for all kinds of animals — a love that can be traced back for generations. Except for spiders, which just terrify me, I have this gene as well, and it is why I am donating a portion of the proceeds from this book to the SPCA International. It's just in us. While my sister was beginning her servitude in the corporate world, she also began volunteering at the National Aquarium in Baltimore, which is often cited as the best aquarium in the world. The work they do there for conservation and education is pretty incredible. Just like me, my sister had grown up in a house full of animals — dogs, cats, hamsters, hermit crabs, goldfish won at a carnival and the occasional baby bird that fell out of a nest. Pretty standard stuff.

The world my sister was volunteering in may as well have been Jurassic Park. In this incredibly unfamiliar world, she was working with sharks, jellyfish, octopus, seals, caimans and one scary-ass Anaconda from the Amazon. It was such a different dynamic and something that she had been curious about for some time but hadn't pursued initially due to her comfort level with the world of Corporate Communications. Yet here she was, volunteering alongside marine biologists, veterinarians and experts in the marine animal behaviors of sharks and dolphins. This was the unfamiliar. Besides those hermit crabs and a goldfish from the carnival, her experience with the underwater world was a futile and unsuccessful attempt at bodyboarding one summer in Ocean City, MD. Unless getting tossed and turned under the waves after multiple wipeouts makes you familiar with marine life, she had a total amount of zero experience.

And now? Well, deciding to embrace the unfamiliar just like our lovable Akeem did wonders for her career growth. She became one of just a few non-marine biologists at the aquarium, and eventually secured a job as an aquarist — prompted by a group of marine-life experts she worked with who successfully lobbied on her behalf. She continued moving forward in her career and was recently promoted to Curator of the Animal Care and Rescue Center. She has spoken at conferences all over the world on topics that I can't even pronounce and has done all of this without a marine biology degree. She is the most perfect example of how putting ourselves in unfamiliar territory can do wonders for our career growth. Yes, I am a proud big bro and no, Ash, you are not getting any royalties from this chapter.

Even with all of the options available, it's easy to get into a groove, find a comfy path and stay on it. Not in the 40-years-and-a-gold-watch sense but we find something we are good at or maybe something that comes easy, and we stick to the plan. If that's what works for you, well then in the words of the poet laureate Rocky Balboa in response to Ivan Drago's "I must break you," then "Go for it."

However, if you are ready to test yourself with the unfamiliar as you seek that career growth, but might be hesitating based on the size of the change it may present, heed the words of the lovable Prince Akeem who said, "No journey is too great when one finds what he seeks."

If you are ready to test yourself with the unfamiliar as you seek that career growth, but might be hesitating based on the size of the change it may present, heed the words of the lovable Prince Akeem who said, "No journey is too great when one finds what he seeks."

CHAPTER 7

BETTER OFF DEAD

**"Go that way really fast. If something
gets in your way, turn."**

Charles De Mar

When we think of '80s movies, one of the first names to come
to mind is John Cusack. He had so many endearing roles —
from the first time we saw him as Bryce (one of the geeks) in
Sixteen Candles to the lovesick kickboxer Lloyd Dobler in *Say
Anything* and everything in-between. He was '80s personified.
When he took on the role of Lane Meyer in *Better Off Dead*,
I don't think anyone would have imagined that his turn as the
jilted ex-boyfriend who tries and fails on multiple occasions to
kill himself would teach us a valuable lesson for the workplace.
Actually, it was his best friend Charles De Mar who uttered the
quote at the top of the chapter that ultimately taught us that:

Sometimes the best way to learn in business is to attack your proverbial "K-12" without a safety net.

Of course, turning slightly to avoid a head-on collision while downhill skiing might allow you to survive for another day, but we will discuss that later. And now that I think about it, I suppose that in Lane's continued attempts at self-annihilation he did teach us never to give up, but we learned that lesson from *The Goonies* in my first book (shameless plug), so we move onward and upward. Now, most of the lessons we learn from '80s movies come from the main characters. But a paperboy named Johnny Gasparini who said roughly 20 words in the entire movie taught us an important business ethics lesson that focuses on: **Paying your vendors on time regardless of the size of the debt.**

So before we make ourselves a little "better off" with our workplace lessons from Lane Meyer and crew, let's harness that 1.88 gigawatts of power and go back to August of 1985.

It was August 23rd to be exact, which was just eight days shy of my 15th birthday, which found me preparing for one more year without the ability to drive myself anywhere, making for the incredibly awkward teenage "dropped off and picked up by Mom" movie date night. Frankly, I'm not sure how much of a date I had that night, considering I spent a good amount of time playing Pac-Man, Galaga and Donkey Kong in the movie theatre lobby. I do recall that my date beat me at all three — handily. The positive in being knocked off my arcade game throne was that she felt sorry for me and let me pick the candy. Mike and Ike's and Hot Tamales if you must know — which even back then cost me substantially more than the price of admission.

Then as the summer was winding down, I was also preparing for my sophomore year of high school with the purchase of a sweet pair of black parachute pants, a striped pair of Jimmy Z Velcro pants, several incredibly colorful Jams printed shirts and a pair of size 13 checkered slip-on Vans, which I can thankfully say are the only fashion brand still left in my current clothing collection from those style-challenged days of '85.

 FUN FACT: Although Vans shoes officially launched as a business in 1966 under the name The Van Doren Rubber Company, it was the Jeff Spicoli character in the 1982 classic *Fast Times at Ridgemont High* who wore the slip-on checkerboard Vans that propelled the brand into the mainstream.

1985 was a fantastic year for entertainment in general, and the music charts were no exception.

1985 was a fantastic year for entertainment in general, and the music charts were no exception. What was incredibly interesting and yet another reason why the '80s delivered pop charts like no other decade before or since, was the impact of movie soundtracks on the Top 40. Sure, we still have the occasional huge song from a movie (like "Let it Go" from *Frozen*, which I've never seen, or more recently "Shallow" from *A Star is*

Born, again which I've never seen). I know, I know. But being a man with no kids equals no *Frozen,* and no current romantic relationship equals no *A Star is Born.* Besides, those movies weren't made in the '80s so they can't be all that good anyway.

Let's get back to 1985, and as Casey Kasem said, "Now on with the countdown." As mentioned before, movie soundtracks were having a huge impact on the charts and this particular week in August was stacked with three in the top 10, including the #1 song "Power of Love" by Huey Lewis and the News (from the movie *Back to the Future).* I do love me some Huey. Coming in at #4 was the theme song to *St. Elmo's Fire, "*Man in Motion" by John Parr and close behind him at #6 was Tina Turner's, "We Don't Need Another Hero" from *Mad Max Beyond Thunderdome.* The '80s had something for everyone. I'd also like to point out that Motley Crue, Depeche Mode, Billy Ocean and Bruce Springsteen were all in the Top 40. My decade wins for musical diversity, and it's not even close.

Although cable television was becoming mainstream in the '80s, we still had an incredibly limited channel selection that was growing slowly after the golden age of rabbit ears television. And although the decade birthed some of the most memorable TV the world has ever seen, television during the summer didn't provide the blockbusters that the movie industry is known for. In fact, it was usually the *Quiet* before the *Riot* (see what I did there) that is the fall lineup. Still, we did have some things happening during the summer of 1985, including the launch of *Nick at Nite,* which, as I've mentioned before (in my first book), gives me my *Friends* fix each evening and the global broadcasting of the incredible Live Aid concerts. We said a tearful goodbye to Richard Dawson — temporarily as it would be — to *Family Feud* and "moved on up" for the last time with *The Jeffersons,* which at 15 years old was a really tough one for me. It was the first time in my television watching career that I really felt like I was losing a close friend who had been in my living room each week for 10 years.

1985 at the box office might have been the greatest year for movies in the '80s, which means it could have been the greatest year ever for movies in history. I mean we are talking about the most influential decade for pop culture in this middle-aged guy's opinion. The weekend that began on August 23rd had enough box office firepower to give John Matrix (played by Arnold Schwarzenegger) in the 1985 *Commando* — whose body count likely made Freddie Krueger jealous — a bit of a pause. *Back to the Future* was #1 after eight weeks in the theatre, which is four times longer than most movie runs today. Another Michael J. Fox-helmed movie, *Teen Wolf,* debuted at #2 while we also found two of the all-time comedic greats — John Candy in *Summer Rental* and Chevy Chase as Clark Griswold in *European Vacation* — keeping their residency intact at the '80s box office. One of the most underrated and entertaining horror movies, *Fright Night,* was just outside of the top 10, followed by Val Kilmer and *Real Genius,* which will definitely have a chapter in my next book. Of course, no top box office list in the '80s would be complete without a Sylvester Stallone entry; in this case: *Rambo: First Blood Part II,* that on that date was moving ever closer to $150 million in sales.

It was a little-heralded debut that same weekend which is the impetus for this chapter.

But it was a little-heralded debut that same weekend which is the impetus for this chapter. *Better Off Dead* directed and written by savage Steve Holland and starring John Cusack, Diane Franklin, David Ogden Stiers, Amanda Wyss and Curtis Armstrong — of *Revenge of the Nerds* and *Risky Business* fame — hit the box office. Over the years, it became the epitome of a cult classic and is often mentioned as one of the great dark comedies of the 1980s. *Better Off Dead* tells the story of Lane Meyer, played by John Cusack, whose girlfriend Beth has dumped him for the town ski stud Roy Stalin who, as you can probably guess, wears a sweater neatly tied around his neck. Throughout the movie, Lane goes back and forth between searching for ways to either kill himself or win back his girlfriend from the horrible, terrible, no-good Roy. Depressed and in despair, Lane decides to commit suicide but fails miserably, as multiple attempts fall short of his goal for a variety of reasons. Lane Meyer is the antithesis of the optimistic Ferris Bueller and the word "can't" is a common go-to for him, although I could relate when he said, "I have a great fear of tools. I once made a birdhouse in woodshop, and the fair housing committee condemned it. I can't." Yes, my trials in woodshop class are well documented.

Ultimately, Lane — along with his friend Charles De Mar (Curtis Armstrong) — decides that the only way he can get his girlfriend Beth to date him again is to beat Roy Stalin in a ski race down the K-12, which is the Mt. Everest of their little town.

Along the way, Lane meets a French foreign exchange student named Monique, played magnificently by Diane Franklin, who is living across the street during her stay in the U.S. Unfortunately, she has been paired with an incredibly awkward mother and son — Mrs. Smith and Ricky — the latter of whom has a huge and rather creepy crush on her. In order to allay his advances, she claims to have no English-speaking skills, which is not true, and when she finally opens up to Lane, he comes to find that not only is she very intelligent, but is also a mechanic and a baseball fan. If you haven't seen the movie (how dare you), then you can probably see where this is going à la the darkish romantic comedy.

FUN FACT: Diane Franklin played Karen in the '80s classic, *The Last American Virgin,* which is one of the most underrated movies of all time. It has the realest ending of any coming-of-age movie and arguably the greatest movie soundtrack of the '80s.

Besides the brilliance that is John Cusack, one of the reasons that *Better Off Dead* has become a cult classic and is oft-quoted even 34 years later, is because of the group of oddballs who make up our little fictional town of Greendale, CA. Oddballs like:

- **Ricky,** the slightly overweight neighbor who fancies himself a stud worthy of the *Top Gun* beach volleyball scene and, as Lane says, "just sits around crocheting all day and snorting nasal spray."

- **Ricky's mom,** who also fancies her son a stud and loves her blue eyeshadow.

- **Charles De Mar**, who is Lane's best friend and provides the quote for our first lesson, exclaiming when looking at the monstrous K-12 ski slope, "This is pure snow! It's everywhere! Do you have any idea what the street value of this mountain is?"

- **The Ree brothers**, who challenge Lane to a race at every stoplight and learned English by listening to Howard Cosell, who they channel before each race against Lane through a megaphone attached to the car which gives us classic lines like "Truly a sight to behold. A man beaten. The once-great champ, now, a study in moppishness."

- **Lane's mom, Jenny**, who often seems lost, and who gives her husband an aardvark costume for Christmas (made of aardvark fur) and thinks that French Fries, French dressing and French bread are, well, French cuisine.

- **Monique Junot**, the beautiful French foreign exchange student and Lane's eventual love interest, who is the optimist to Lane's pessimist and an expert auto mechanic but struggles with English word translation ... specifically the difference in meaning between testicles and tentacles.

- Finally, we have **Johnny Gasparini**, the newspaper boy with the ever-popular '80s switchblade comb who takes his job of collecting the "two dollars ... cash" for his route seriously and teaches us a valuable lesson along the way.

So what did Lane Meyer and his group of Greendale, CA, oddballs teach us about today's workplace?

Sometimes the best way to learn in business is to attack your proverbial "K-12" without a safety net.

As mentioned above, the K-12 was the mountain peak in the small ski town of Greendale, CA, that only the very best of the best could conquer. Lane's nemesis, Roy Stalin who stole his girlfriend, was the captain of the ski team and someone who had conquered the K-12. And just for posterity's sake, I would like to mention again that he wore his sweater tied around his neck. I think I need to go see a hypnotist to figure out why I loathe that so much. Nah. We all loathe it, don't we?

During this mental struggle, he finds himself so frustrated that he makes the mistake of challenging Roy to a race down the K-12, which he gladly accepts. Of course, Lane wants to keep the bet strictly between them, but as high school would have it, the intercom blasts the next day: "This just in. Lane Meyer will be racing Roy Stalin down K-12 this Sunday at noon." No turning back now.

Just to give you an idea of the lack of confidence that Lane had in himself to accomplish anything successfully and why Monique was such a perfect partner for him, consider this conversation they had earlier in the movie:

> **Lane:** "I have a great fear of tools. I once made a birdhouse in woodshop, and the fair housing committee condemned it. I can't."
>
> **Monique:** "'I cannot do it' is your middle name."

At the time of the announcement, Lane is sitting with Monique, and he says to her, "I must be brain-damaged. I'm gonna race. I'm gonna lose. And I'm gonna die." Now as an entrepreneur or someone appointed to your first leadership role or even someone chasing an idea that you sometimes think might be a little crazy, you've probably had a similar thought go through your head. I know I have. But once you've made the commitment to yourself or others, it's time to make every effort to deliver. And just like Lane, we don't always have a plan before we put ourselves out there. As one of my favorite people, Sir Richard Branson, said:

> *"If somebody offers you an amazing opportunity, but you are not sure you can do it, say yes and then learn how to do it later!"*

At the time of the announcement, Lane is sitting with Monique, and he says to her, "I must be brain-damaged. I'm gonna race. I'm gonna lose. And I'm gonna die."

Of course, Lane wasn't offered an opportunity by someone else — no, he did a great job of putting himself right into his very own proverbial pickle. But the sentiment is the same, and he most certainly had to learn how to do it later, so let's welcome back his best friend Charles De Mar to help us with our first lesson.

When Charles says, "Go that way really fast. If something gets in your way, turn," he is doing his level best to encourage Lane as he stands at the top of the terrifying K-12 peak for the first time. Not exactly the words of encouragement that one wants to hear in that situation, but when faced with the unknown and no time to plan, it's really the best advice one can receive.

Let's think about this in terms of business or your career. If you want to be successful, you will likely be in a position at some point where you will have to "get out over your skis" a bit and take a chance. And if you are an entrepreneur, it's more likely that it will be two or three or four. Oftentimes these chances, may have an educated-guess philosophy of sorts, but there will also be times when you really just need to go in blind, unsure of what might get in your way or when it's time to turn. For example, your competition may already be ahead of you or they may have the resources that you don't to help them plan and move faster. In this situation, you don't have time to plot out your route. By the time you do, they may have already conquered that peak and moved on to the next one. In this case, you'll need to trust your inner toolkit — instinct, intuition, intelligence, determination, guts — and "Go that way really fast" without the idea of a safety net to hold you back or make you think about what happens if you fall. You need to trust yourself and believe in your ability to beat Roy Stalin's ass to the bottom of the mountain regardless of his experience, time to plan and familiarity with the route. Strap in, drop in, get creative, figure out the path as you go and follow the advice of the magnificent Robert Frost when he said:

"Two woods diverged in a wood, and I —
I took the one less traveled by,
And that has made all the difference."

And if nothing else, at the end of the day, you can say that you read a book that found a way to attempt to teach you a business lesson combining advice from Sir Richard Branson, Robert Frost and the noted '80s philosopher Charles De Mar.

Always pay your vendors on time.

When we are introduced to the switchblade comb-carrying newspaper boy, Johnny Gasparini, he is attempting to collect a small, simple debt from the Lane Meyer residence for services rendered. That service being newspaper delivery. He knocks on the door, and the conversation goes like this:

Lane: "Johnny ..."

Johnny: "Four weeks, 20 papers, that's two dollars plus tip."

Lane: "Gee, Johnny, I don't have a dime."

Johnny: "Didn't ask for a dime. Two dollars."

Lane: "Well ... it's funny see ... my mom had to leave early to take my brother to school and my dad to work ..."

Johnny: "Two dollars ... cash."

Lane: "See, the problem here is that my little brother, this morning, got his arm caught in the microwave and um my grandmother dropped acid, and she freaked out, and hijacked a school bus full of penguins, so it's kind of a family crisis...so come back later? Great."

And Lane shuts the door in Johnny's face. Not exactly what they teach you in Business Ethics 101, and this only prompts Johnny to take his bill collecting to the next level. As if inspired by the words of John Rambo when he said, "They drew first blood. Not me," he first gathers all the other newspaper route kids to chase

Lane through the woods in the middle of the night, screaming for their two dollars. Later he jumps on the roof of Lane's car and pounds on the windshield while screaming for his "two dollars ... cash" as Lane tries to drive away. Hey, listen, two dollars in 1985 went a very long way — eight games of Galaga in the arcade, four bags of Big League Chew bubblegum, two movie rentals at the local video store provided you didn't get the "forgot to rewind fee" or even one movie ticket minus the popcorn and soda.

Back to Lane, our paperboy and his two dollars ... cash. Lane's story about his grandmother dropping acid and hijacking a school bus full of penguins is both funny and outlandish, but his attempt to avoid paying his vendor for services rendered is all too common, particularly when those vendors are small or solo freelance shops. This isn't cool at all. When I asked one of my freelancer friends to describe in '80s terms what it was like sometimes trying to get paid for his services, he threw out a few lyrics from the alt-pop band Dead or Alive when they sang:

> *"You spin me right round, baby, right round.*
> *Like a record, baby, right round, right round."*

In the first chapter, we learned a lesson from *The Outsiders* about our moral and ethical compasses through the idea of "staying gold." One of the cornerstones of those compasses would be to pay your debts on time and to avoid contracting for services unless you know you will have the ability to pay for them. It seems pretty simple, and unlike many of our business lessons, our initial introduction to it starts when we are very young with something like a pinkie swear after a bet is made with the winner receiving the agreed-upon prize, which in my case was probably a frozen Snickers bar at the community pool.

 FUN FACT: Although the pinky swear has existed in the US since around 1860, it is thought to have started in Japan where the agreement is sometimes confirmed with "Finger cut-off, ten thousand fist-punchings, whoever lies has to swallow a thousand needles."[1]

Who knows, maybe if the punishment for not paying your vendors on time was swallowing a thousand needles, it would be rare indeed but just a cursory search on Twitter using "not paying vendors" results in a huge number of tweets from mostly freelancers and small to mid-size businesses. As a former head of marketing for 20-plus years, I've hired a lot of vendors, mostly good with a few interesting ones thrown in. But regardless of the results, as long as the good faith effort was there, I would be on the phone with accounting the minute that we missed the agreed-to terms for payment. Making sure that we held up our end of the contract will always be a hill that I am willing to die on. Maybe I'm so die-hard about paying my vendors because I grew up with a dad who was an entrepreneur who built businesses from the ground up and had to chase payments constantly. I saw the frustration and angst that it causes.

---

1 https://en.wikipedia.org/wiki/Pinky_swear and
   https://en.wikipedia.org/wiki/Daijirin

*Maybe I'm so die-hard about paying
my vendors because I grew up with
a dad who was an entrepreneur who
built businesses from the ground up and
had to chase payments constantly.*

As the businesses you work for get bigger, so do the processes, and it becomes easier to find that a payment was "lost in the shuffle" or perhaps one of the 30 steps weren't done correctly which then prompted a non-payment. Whatever the case, not paying your vendors on time doesn't just have an external impact, as ultimately you can be seen as the purveyor of non-payment and not the company that you represent. And as you build your career, you will be surprised by the paths that continue to cross throughout the years. It's impressive how small the business world actually is and how quickly titles and fortunes can change.

 DIGRESSION ALERT: Whenever I see the words small and world that close to each other, I have immediate flashbacks of the time that I was on the "It's a Small World" ride at Disney and it broke down about halfway through. We were stuck for almost an hour and the dolls wouldn't stop singing. It was both mind-melting and terrifying. I still wake up screaming.

One more thought on our lesson from Johnny Gasparini, the switchblade comb-carrying paperboy. As I mentioned before, paying vendors on time is a hill that I will most certainly die on, and when something has been out of my control, I've always communicated with the vendor every step of the way. There may even be times where I've potentially put my job on the line by fighting so hard for something that should be so simple. But I believe strongly in fulfilling the obligation that resulted from your workplace pinkie swear. Throughout my journey to transform myself into a speaker and author in recent years, I've worked with a lot of freelancers and solo practitioners, and they have all been amazing. With each and every partnership, I've made it my number-one priority to pay them under the terms set, and unlike a larger business, I don't negotiate costs. I want them to earn a fair wage for their time, and I want them to receive that wage on time. Period. Because of this simple philosophy, I have watched people go above and beyond to do their part to help me succeed. An extra hour here or an additional service there can result in a "Don't worry about it. I'm happy to help you with this." Everybody wins and isn't that what it is supposed to be about?

> *An extra hour here or an additional service*
> *there can result in a "Don't worry about*
> *it. I'm happy to help you with this."*

Building a stable foundation of clients is how freelancers and small businesses succeed and thrive. Repeat business is absolutely essential for their growth. Building a stable foundation of vendors will help you succeed, whether it's with your existing position, a new career, or the building of a business or brand. Knowing you have trusted experts ready to jump in and help you drive business or look amazing in front of a new boss will give you peace of mind.

Lessons in leadership, management style and how to a grow
a business may change and evolve over the years, but the way
we define respect and integrity will be the same long after our
"Living Years" as the band Mike and The Mechanics sang back
in 1988. So don't make your vendors chase you through a park
in the middle of the night screaming for their "two dollars …
cash." Pay them on time. It's the right thing to do.

> *So don't make your vendors chase you through*
> *a park in the middle of the night screaming for*
> *their "two dollars … cash." Pay them on time.*

CHAPTER 8

WEIRD SCIENCE

"You had to be big shots, didn't you? You had to show off. When are you gonna learn that people will like you for who you are, not for what you can give them."

Lisa, *Weird Science*

When an entrepreneur, inventor or a forward-thinking businessperson hears something like "that is the craziest idea ever" or "that will never work," it is often more fuel on the fire. I mean, after all, if what they were proposing was "normal," someone would have done it before. It takes a bit of crazy to continue to move the business world forward and if "necessity is the mother of invention," then maybe curiosity — or crazy — is the mother of innovation.

But just like when the high school outcasts Gary and Wyatt in *Weird Science* decided to use Wyatt's home computer circa

1985 to create what in their 17-year-old, not-fully-evolved minds constituted the perfect woman, all of us who love to innovate must always be mindful of one very important thing: **Your craziest idea may just work. Be prepared or face the consequences.** And face the consequences they did, as we will discuss later in this chapter.

Speaking of computers, how many times in the past year have you had to contact an IT person for assistance? It's the world we live in and as Benjamin Franklin said, "In this world, nothing can be said to be certain except death, taxes ... and our ever-growing need for IT support." Okay, so that last part is a bit of a modern interpretation, but I'm sure Ben would need it as much as anyone if he were here today. The reality is that the only person in a business today who escapes the need for an IT person is the IT person. And, of course, you know that they know, you know?

Lisa, the woman who our two knuckleheads created, is the strongest and smartest character in the movie for a number of reasons that we will review later in this chapter. And because she was essentially created through the use of a computer, she could also be considered a bit of an IT person herself. As we will also learn from Lisa, it is very important to **make friends with the IT person because they can make you look like a superhero or a pile of shit.**

So, before we find out if these business lessons are more "weird" or "science" (I think the latter, of course), let's *Time Bandits* this thing and go back once again to August of 1985. August 2nd to be exact.

During our childhood, early August may have signaled that the new school year was rapidly approaching, but it was also when the days seemed the longest and the night sky revealed its most majestic display of celestial bodies. It was under this night sky that all the kids in my neighborhood played games like kick the can, ghost in the graveyard and Marco Polo. After 8:00 p.m. on any given night during this time of summer, you would hear "Ally, ally oxen free" or "Come out, come out, wherever you are" and then see no less than 15 kids come out from their hiding places to gather around the can that had just been kicked, signifying that all were free to reveal themselves. At the time, none of us really knew that this would be the last summer of these neighborhood games, as half us would secure our driver's licenses over the next year and Marco Polo would be replaced with cruisin' the mall parking lot.

This was also the summer that I worked at WaveDancer surf shop, ironically named, as the closest waves were a solid three-hour drive away. Initially, I was a salesperson and proudly recall the first time that I was secret-shopped. For those of you who have never worked in retail, secret shoppers are hired by the store to pose as regular customers and evaluate the salespeople for things like service, knowledge and overall professionalism. Later I found out that my secret shoppers were a couple looking for wetsuits, who I ultimately upgraded to masks and fins along with their purchase of two O'Neill full-body wetsuits. I passed with flying colors and finally got promoted to the skateboard area, which made me the coolest guy in the shop. I wasn't though, not by a long shot, but hey, just like Ray said in the classic *Ghostbusters,* "When someone asks if you are a God, you say, yes!" And as you probably saw in the table of contents, we will most certainly get to some Ghostbusting lessons before the end of this book.

Working in a surf shop was super cool on a number of levels, including the music that we piped into the store. The mid-'80s and specifically 1985 was an amazing time for the alternative genre that was in its relative infancy. The emo of today was the goth of yesteryear, and their influence on the alt scene was strong. Three of the most influential alt bands of the '80s — The Cure, The Smiths and New Order — released albums titled *The Head on the Door*, *Meat is Murder* and *Low-Life*, respectively. In most of my chapters, I pepper you with a few songs from that particular moment of the '80s I'm discussing, but these albums are amazing from Side A to Side B and back again so picking one song from each would be blasphemous. R.E.M., Simple Minds, Sonic Youth, The Red Hot Chili Peppers and The Clash also released incredible music in '85 but the one that I still crank up in my house today is The Cult album titled *Love*. Thank you WaveDancer surf shop for bringing Ian Astbury and the boys into my life.

One area of television history that I haven't explored all that much was the influence of MTV at a certain point during the '80s. Yes, before *Jersey Shore*, *16 and Pregnant* and *Teen Mom OG*, MTV actually played music videos.

FUN FACT: The first music video ever played on MTV was "Video Killed the Radio Star" by The Buggles at 12:01 a.m. on August 1, 1981. The original five VJs were Nina Blackwood, Mark

Goodman, Alan Hunter, J.J. Jackson and
Martha Quinn.

**ANOTHER FUN FACT: In the video, there is
a brief shot of a man wearing black and playing
the keyboard. That man is Hans Zimmer, who
went on to compose music for more than 150
films, including *Gladiator*, *The Dark Knight
Trilogy* and *The Lion King*, for which he won an
Academy Award for Best Original Score.**

~~~~~~

As we've discussed before, summers tended to be a little
slow for television back in the three-network-channels and
basic-cable-package decade of the '80s. So I thought it would
be fun to reflect back on some of the top MTV videos during the
summer of 1985. Duran Duran's "A View to a Kill," the theme
song to the James Bond movie by the same name, integrated
big-budgeted action scenes from the movie with an incredibly
smooth Roger Moore and low-budget special effects with the
incredibly mullet-strong Simon Le Bon. Motley Crue appeared
in a bathroom mirror and pulled a bullied kid through it into
the world that could be his if he would just do a little "Smoking
in the Boys Room." And there was Prince, whose magic could
even make a video that was highlighted by clouds, balloons and
kaleidoscope-style special effects look cooler than cool with
"Raspberry Beret."

At the box office, 1985 was in one word: incredible. The
weekend of August 2nd brought us movies with Chevy Chase,
Sylvester Stallone, Mel Gibson, Clint Eastwood and Michael
J. Fox. The Griswolds were doing their best impression of

ridiculous in *European Vacation* while Stallone was delivering
an '80s-action movie body count in *Rambo: First Blood Part
II.* Mad Max was going apocalyptic in *Beyond Thunderdome*
while everyone's favorite bad-ass cowboy Eastwood was taking
advantage of a nice piece of hickory in *Pale Rider.* At #1 in the
box office once again was Marty McFly and Doc Brown in *Back
to the Future.*

The movie for our workplace lessons in this chapter, *Weird
Science,* was sitting at #4 at the box office coming into its
first full weekend. Directed and written by the masterful
John Hughes and starring Anthony Michael Hall, Ilan
Mitchell-Smith, Kelly LeBrock and Bill Paxton, it told the
story of two unpopular high school boys who decide to create
a woman using their computer. Gary (played by Hall) and
Wyatt (played by Smith) are on a mission to be accepted by
the popular crowd and the student population in general.
As immature high school boys are wont to do, they devise an
insane, ridiculous and not-at-all-thought-out plan to solve
their problem. In this case, they believe that creating a beautiful
woman to accompany them to events and parties will boost
their profile with other kids who will accept them into the
clique, and all will be right in their universe.

The woman they create, Lisa (played by Kelly LeBrock), is
beautiful — as they had hoped — but more importantly
she has a genius-level intelligence (they did scan a copy of
Einstein's brain into her profile), — a quick wit, superpowers
that she uses to quell the obnoxious and a desire to really teach
the boys how to become upstanding men. She is by far the
strongest character in the movie and provides a very different

perspective to the movie than the poster would suggest. She plays a very big role in our lessons, as you will see.

Throughout the movie, the two boys are tormented by Wyatt's older brother Chet, played by the gone-way-too-soon Bill Paxton, and by your typical most-popular-guy-in-high-school knucklehead Ian, played by a very young and not-yet-known Robert Downey, Jr. Both of them do their best to keep the boys from gaining any semblance of self-confidence through embarrassing them with things like dumping shakes on them at a crowded mall just as Wyatt is saying to Gary, "You know for the first time in my life I don't feel like a total dick," de-pantsing them in front of gym class and consistent verbal beatdowns at every turn.

Lisa does her best to teach them how to be men, and in the process, she finds very impressive and hilarious ways to teach their tormentors the lessons that they so aptly deserve — one of which will teach us a lesson for the workplace. Through her "superpowers," she provides them with all the outward-facing tools that they need to be "cool" — fashion-able clothes, fancy cars, better haircuts and a well-marketed party at Wyatt's house. All these things certainly help with expediting their journey to acceptance, but it is really the way she creates situations that teach them to be self-confident, which ultimately leads to the growth they really needed, thus prompting her to say, "I'm just really getting off seeing you guys straightened out."

FUN FACT: The theme song for *Weird Science*, "It's a Dead Man's Party," was performed by Oingo Boingo and written by their lead singer Danny Elfman (who is a prolific music composer for the big screen). He has four Academy Award nominations for *Good Will Hunting, Men in Black, Big Fish* and *Milk.* He also composed the theme for *The Simpsons,* which is the longest-running American sitcom and the longest-running scripted U.S. primetime television series.

So what did Gary, Wyatt and Lisa teach us about today's workplace?

 Your craziest idea may just work. Be prepared, or face the consequences.

When Gary and Wyatt sit down at Wyatt's computer to create a real-live woman, Dr. Frankenstein-style, they aren't expecting it to actually work. Unlike the classic Mary Shelley novel, they thankfully did not have to rob graves to piece together their creation. They were able to cut things out of magazines, encyclopedias (look that word up if you are under 30 — it was essentially Google masquerading as a volume of hardback books) and their high school textbooks, which were all scanned-in to create a profile. They even hooked up a Barbie doll and ran electric currents through it, hoping to jumpstart their efforts. Juvenile? Yes. Stupid? Yes. Crazy? Yes. But it worked. And now that their craziest idea just became a reality, they have to figure out what to do next.

They were unprepared and hurtling quickly toward a multitude of consequences for their lack of planning. But can you blame them for a lack of preparedness? Just attempting this stunt was crazy enough but actually believing that it would work would be, in the words of Ozzy Osbourne, *"... going off the rails on a crazy train."* The consequences they ultimately endure range from the silly to the absurd to the downright terrifying. First and foremost, they aren't even sure how to act around a woman and quickly become awkward and uncomfortable any time she is around, prompting her to say, "If we're going to have any fun together, you guys had better learn how to loosen up."

As they become more comfortable and more willing to "loosen up," their lack of planning and preparation really comes to the forefront: Wyatt's brother, Chet, who is already an obnoxious blowhard with an affinity for bullying those weaker than him, begins realizing that something is going on and says, "I'm gonna tell Mom and Dad everything. I'm even considering making up some shit." In this case, payoffs of a sort are required for him to move on from his threats; Lisa confronts Gary's dad over his refusal to allow him to go to a party with her that turns into a cavalcade of verbal abuse and insults from Lisa, including "Don't threaten me, Al! You're out of shape. I'll kick your arse." Gary, of course, goes into full-on panic mode about how his parents are going to ground him until he is 45; a massive missile appears in Wyatt's house with the tip crashing through the roof; a motorcycle gang shows up at their party driving their bikes through the house and destroying everything in sight; Wyatt's grandparents are put into a catatonic state by

Lisa and then placed in the kitchen closet; Chet comes home to find that it is snowing in his room; and while hiding from the biker gang, Gary and Wyatt are discovered and humiliated in front of the entire party for being cowards. I should add that this is just a partial list of the consequences from their significant lack of preparedness and planning.

So, what does this mean for the workplace today? We've all heard the phrase "break through the clutter," and, of course, the buzziest of buzzwords over the past few years, "disruptive." Both consumers and B2B customers have a constant barrage of messages, services, products and ideas thrown at them every day, which is why these phrases exist. Today, where a product, service or business can be introduced to the world within a matter of seconds and with the potential to dismantle a century-old industry in months, the crazy idea is often the one that is needed but unfortunately not embraced.

Crazy is the mother of innovation. I mean, think about it — just in the past 12 years or so, we've had crazy ideas not just become a reality, but in some instances drastically change the way we live our lives. Who would have thought that a camera would be a necessity for a phone? Crazy. Who would have thought that millions of people every day would get into a stranger's private car (not a licensed taxi) to get from point A to point B? Crazy. Who would have thought that we can send a rocket into space to deliver a payload and then have it return nicely and neatly right back from where it was launched? Crazy. Who would have thought that selling books online would turn into a trillion-dollar business? Crazy. Who would have thought that almost every person on the planet would gladly share their preferences for everything, all of their thoughts and their entire life — past, present, future — with the rest of the world through products that don't give you anything tangible in return except the acknowledgment of others? Crazy.

All these ideas and a much longer list were likely labeled as crazy, but they worked. And they didn't just work — they changed the world forever. In this book, we won't get into the specifics of who did what, but if you have just a cursory interest in the business world (I'm imagining that you do) then you know very well, which of these unnamed companies above were not prepared for their craziest idea to work, and ultimately faced some pretty daunting consequences à la Gary and Wyatt. Thankfully, each of those same companies also had a "Lisa" who was able to take control of the situation and save them from themselves.

Even some of our great 21st-century visionaries and inventors, like Elon Musk — who founded the company SpaceX, which launches rockets into orbit that incredibly land back in the same spot from which they launched — has had his well-documented Gary and Wyatt "crazy idea that worked" moments with Tesla, the electric car company he launched way back in 2003.

Sometimes, a company faces the consequences of not having a plan for when their competition's craziest idea actually works. One of the best examples of this was back in 2007 when Steve Ballmer, then CEO of Microsoft, was interviewed about the recent launch of the iPhone by Steve Jobs at Macworld. Ballmer is easily one of the most successful business people in American history, and his legacy in the technology space is set securely in stone, but his response to a question about the iPhone and Microsoft's Zune is interesting and likely regrettable:[1]

> **Interviewer**: "Zune was getting some traction, then Steve Jobs goes to Macworld, and he pulls out this iPhone. What was your first reaction when you saw that?"

> **Ballmer**: (Laughing) "500 dollars! Fully subsidized with a plan? I said that is the most expensive phone in the world and it doesn't appeal to business customers because it doesn't have a keyboard, which makes it not a very good email machine."

Oh, Lisa, where art thou? Even the best and the brightest can be guilty of labeling the crazy idea unsustainable and ultimately foregoing a plan or preparations for when it actually works. iPhone? Zune? As one my dad's favorites, Paul Harvey, said, "And now you know the rest of the story."

So, encourage the crazy ideas in your workplace, on your team or in your head. Just make sure you have a plan for when the craziest one works and make sure it's solid. You may not be lucky enough to have a Lisa. After all, anyone can make a plan and as Russell Ziskey (played by the late, great Harold Ramis) said in the 1981 movie *Stripes,* "Custer had a plan, too."

 Make friends with the I.T. person because they can make you look like a superhero or a pile of shit.

---

1   https://bgr.com/2016/11/04/ballmer-iphone-quote-explained/ and
https://fortune.com/2017/01/10/steve-ballmer-apple-iphone/

Two simple letters — I.T. No not E.T. although I know a lot of I.T. people who would gladly give up everything to see the inside of that spaceship that took him home. And because we live in a world where "IT" is a psycho killer clown from the awesome imagination of Stephen King (notably, IT Chapter Two, the sequel, was released as this book was being edited), we will also refer to our information technology friends as I.T. with two periods.

I'm hoping it is obvious at this point that Lisa is one of my favorite characters from '80s movies, and that is saying a lot. She is the strongest and most powerful character in the movie, and it isn't even close. She has a genius-level intelligence that she uses judiciously; she has an incredibly quick wit that is on display multiple times; she is a master problem solver; she is always several steps ahead of everyone else; and she does not suffer fools and absolutely crushes obnoxious "bro dudes" verbally, emotionally and physically even altering their appearance when necessary. And that is the one attribute that we will focus on for this chapter.

When Lisa meets Wyatt's older brother, Chet, it is easy to see why she has a pure disdain for his entire being. He is the very definition of obnoxious and spends his days parading around as if the entire world should be thankful for his presence. Sound like a familiar personality in your workplace? His approach to everyone, particularly Gary and Wyatt, is to dismantle their entire being through insults, threats and blackmail. And it works. It's clear from the beginning of the movie that Wyatt, his younger brother, has already succumbed to his daily beatdowns and it is certainly clear in this exchange (the morning after they come back from a night of partying):

Wyatt: "I don't have the bucks to pay Chet off about this."

Gary: "You can't fear Chet for the rest of your life."

Wyatt: "Why not?"

Enter Lisa. The moment that Chet lays eyes on her, he uses his tactics that have worked so well on everyone else, but as we learned before, she suffers no fools. He offends her early and often with obnoxious advances, and questions her intelligence, and her judgment. And when he is alone with her in the house, he dials up his most egregious pickup line while refusing to heed her request to back off of Wyatt and Gary. She warns him, and he responds with "Hit me with your best shot," which I'd like to think was a John Hughes nod to the 1980 Pat Benatar smash hit.

Hit him she does, by turning him into a living, breathing and talking pile of shit complete with an appetite for the very flies that surround him. It's well-deserved, of course, and the only way out of this predicament is to apologize to his brother Wyatt for all of the things he has done to him.

So now the question is, what is the connection to I.T. through all of this? I'm glad you asked. Lisa was created from a computer, so for our purposes, she is most certainly an I.T. person. I mean, honestly, besides Joshua in the 1983 box office hit *WarGames,* there really isn't a better example from the '80s movies of a character that is more closely tied to computers and how they work. Perhaps, Wormser from *Revenge of the Nerds* in a different and less powerful way.

So now the question is, what is the connection to I.T. through all of this? I'm glad you asked. Lisa was created from a computer, so for our purposes, she is most certainly an I.T. person. I mean, honestly, besides Joshua in the 1983 box office hit **WarGames***, there really isn't a better example from the '80s movies of a character that is more closely tied to computers and how they work.*

Of all the departments or people that you rely on for support to do your job, which one has the biggest impact on your ability to be successful? If you answered I.T., then you know what it is like to have to call for help when a program freezes, a presentation that you've worked on for days is lost and "unrecoverable" hours before your meeting, your VPN isn't working rendering you useless on a remote day, you opened an email that you shouldn't have and fear you may have infected the company's systems (you know you've done it) or the error message window keeps popping up again and again and again. This list could literally go on forever, but the point is that as connected and integrated as we are with technology today, no company or employee can be successful without a strong I.T. person or group.

Most of the time, when we have to make the call to I.T. support, we are either frustrated or in a full-on panic mode, which makes for a stressful situation right from the start. Whatever our problem is, we need it resolved quickly, and we can't do it ourselves. It's certainly understandable, but the person on the other end is the one preparing to don a cape for you and turn a failure into a potential success.

Here is where it gets real for all of us:

Just like Lisa, I.T. professionals have the ability to make you look like a superhero — as she did with Gary and Wyatt — or a pile of live fly-eating shit à la Chet. They legitimately have this super-power, and they know it.

Almost every problem you will encounter with your software or hardware is solvable by most I.T. people. Some issues will take time and will require them to shift some priorities around while others can be resolved in minutes or sometimes seconds, like the famous "have you rebooted or restarted your computer since you first noticed this problem?" (It's amazing how many times that actually works.) However, most issues will require some sort of problem-solving from I.T., so the tone you set from the beginning can often dictate your priority level for the issue today and in the future.

When most people start at a new company, they are eager to get introduced to the leaders. They seek them out and begin positioning themselves for access to the best opportunities within the group. Understandable, of course, but I take a very different course of action. I find the I.T. team as quickly as I can, introduce myself and compliment them on the work they do behind the scenes to contribute to the success of the company. As an added bonus, it also helps to have the 1984 Whodini hit song "Friends" playing in the background as well:

"Friends
How many of us have them?
Friends.
Ones we can depend on."

I take a very different course of action.
I find the I.T. team as quickly as I can,
introduce myself and compliment them
on the work they do behind the scenes to
contribute to the success of the company.

Call it what you like, but there are departments that get too much credit when things go well and ones that tend only to be recognized when something goes wrong. I.T. is in the latter group, and everyone digs a compliment.

At the end of the day, I would much rather be a superhero than a smelly pile of excrement, and since Lisa has returned to the virtual world, I know exactly who can help make that happen.

CHAPTER 9

GHOSTBUSTERS

"Why worry? Each one of us is carrying an unlicensed nuclear accelerator on his back."

Dr. Peter Venkman, *Ghostbusters*

As we move through life, most of us naturally become less risk-averse. Where we were invincible in our youth, we now begin to discover our own mortality through life events and situations. The idea of being a little more cautious as we gain more wisdom isn't a bad thing, but it will begin to limit our ability to grow. Oftentimes, this is the situation that really big global businesses find themselves in and, while they are spending time cautiously evaluating and weighing the potential risks of their next move, a smaller and leaner competitor is strapping unlicensed nuclear accelerators to their backs and growing their business by ridding a terrified city of ghosts and poltergeists. Okay, so maybe they aren't modern-day ghost hunters or even Ghostbusters like Dr. Peter Venkman, Dr. Raymond Stantz, Dr. Egon Spengler and Winston Zeddemere, but entrepreneurs and strong corporate leaders realize that **the best accelerant for business growth is risk.** Of course, outfitting yourself with an unlicensed nuclear pack may be too much of a "kickstart to your heart" (as Motley Crue said in their 1989 hit) but being universally risk-averse will result in stagnation, which is a really ugly word for any business.

> *Of course, outfitting yourself with an unlicensed nuclear pack may be too much of a "kickstart to your heart" (as Motley Crue said in their 1989 hit) but being universally risk-averse will result in stagnation, which is a really ugly word for any business.*

For most of us, our careers are not going to be a straight-line, void of the bumps and sometimes bruises that our lives tend to provide every so often as a reminder to us that the majority of the time we have it pretty good. Venkman, Stantz and Egon take a significant bruising early in the movie when their grant is terminated, and they are fired from Columbia University, where they are employed as scientists studying the asexual mating habits of plants and flowers. I'm kidding — just seeing if you are paying attention. They actually study the paranormal, which, of course, makes sense with the whole Ghostbusters thing.

Some of the greatest influencers, icons and business people have been fired at some point in their careers: J.K. Rowling, Jerry Seinfeld, Mark Cuban, Steve Jobs, Oprah Winfrey and Walt Disney.

FUN FACT: Walt Disney was fired from his job as a cartoonist at the *Kansas City Star* because, according to his editor, he "lacked imagination and had no good ideas." Alrighty then.

But as I suppose many of these titans would tell you, **being fired can sometimes be your biggest promotion**. Thankfully, this was certainly true of our goofy but brilliant paranormal professors; otherwise, a small business called Ghostbusters would have ceased to exist. I don't know about you, but having to deal with possessed Stay Puft Marshmallow Men is not a world I want to live in.

So, before we get into the details of what our busters of ghosts taught us for the workplace, let's hit that connecting hook at 88 mph and travel back to early summer 1984.

It was June of 1984, and my middle school years were officially in the rearview mirror. Freshman year of high school was just a few months away, and I was both completely unprepared and a bit naïve as to what this upgrade in the cafeteria food and school supply store actually meant. For those of you who didn't have a school supply store, it was basically a shop inside of the school where you could buy everything from paper and notebooks to scratch-and sniff-stickers and really cool pencil-top erasers in the shape of aliens, sports equipment and cartoon characters. If you need an '80s movie that will give you more insight into this long-gone phenomenon, go watch *Three O'Clock High*, which is an incredibly underrated dark comedy.

Eighth grade at Franklin Middle School meant I was at the top of the food chain and had the respect that came with being an elder statesman. Respect being fleeting, as one misstep, say like slipping and falling while moonwalking at the Autumn sock hop, or having to wear a mock turtleneck while singing "Aquarius" in the choir. could set you back several years in accumulated cool points. Not that I would know about either of the above examples. In actuality, I would later get removed from said choir for foregoing the official choir uniform at a school event for a pair of Georgetown Hoya sweatpants and matching shirt. Original gangster indeed.

Freshman year of high school meant essentially navigating the same size hallways but with very different results. In just one summer, you went from *Coming to America's* "King Jaffe Joffer, ruler of Zamunda" to a "neo maxi zoom dweebie," the classic '80s insult made famous by John Bender in *The Breakfast Club.* Very few escaped this transformation, although some were much quicker than others to move on from it (and notes from your mom that fell out from within your bagged lunch never helped).

That summer between middle school and high school was also when I really began to develop my own tastes in entertainment. It was a really great time for that evolution. In music, the Top 40 was as interesting as ever and was as random as the cards you would get in a pack of Garbage Pail Kids. Cyndi Lauper was at the top of the chart with one of my secret favorites "Time After Time," while the David Lee Roth-led, *Van Halen* wasn't far behind with "I'll Wait." As the '80s was keen to do, we had several one-hit wonders on the charts, including Icicle Works awesome alt/pop song "Whisper to a Scream" and, of course, no Top 40 in the '80s would be complete without an entry from the man himself, Prince, whose "When Doves Cry" was in its 36th week on the charts.

 FUN FACT: David Lee Roth trained as an EMT in New York City during the late 1990s and went on several hundred ambulance rides.

On television, most of America was still reeling from series finales in the prior month that included *Happy Days, Hart to Hart, One Day at a Time* and *Fantasy Island.* Today, we could just tune into the reruns on a multitude of channels or streaming services, but back in the early '80s syndication and reruns were not as easy to come by, so people often felt a part of them go with a show when it ended. The world had also recently lost Andy Kaufman, an eccentric and supremely talented comedian who was known to most as Latka on the hit show *Taxi.* On the bright side, we were still being entertained throughout the week with an invitation to *The Love Boat*; chasing bad guys in Hawaii with *Magnum P.I.* and the best mustache this side of Sam Elliott; drinking beers with Sam Malone and the crew at *Cheers*, and wondering what Willis was talking about in *Different Strokes.*

At the box office, the new PG-13 rating was on the horizon, due to a bit of outrage over scenes in the PG-rated movie *Indiana Jones and The Temple of Doom.* (A few months later *Red Dawn* with my man Patrick Swayze would be the first movie with a PG-13 rating). Beyond Indy doing his thing with his whip and some snark, we were also being entertained by a bunch of light-hating, water-loving, eating-after-midnight mogwais in *Gremlins,* which I will argue is absolutely a Christmas movie. Personally, I was learning the newest poppin' and breakin' moves in *Beat Street* and one of the greatest sports movies of all time, *The Natural,* was hitting a home run at the box office. Okay, that was bad, but I'm allowed a cheesy pun here and there. I mean, I did wear parachute pants at one point in my life, so let me have that one.

And at the top of the box office was *Ghostbusters,* directed by Ivan Reitman and starring Bill Murray, Dan Aykroyd, Harold Ramis, Sigourney Weaver, Ernie Hudson and Rick Moranis. It tells the story of three parapsychology professors — Spengler (Ramis), Venkman (Murray) and Stantz (Aykroyd) — who lose their jobs at Columbia University and go into business for themselves as *The Ghostbusters* to rid New York City of their ever-increasing problem with ghosts, spirits and demons. Along the way, they pick up a fourth buster of ghosts Winston Zeddemere, and a receptionist Janine played by Annie Potts. This is the team that will ultimately have to tussle with two normal citizens who will soon be possessed by demons: a mild-mannered accountant named Louis Tully, played by Rick Moranis, and a classical musician, Dana Barrett, played by Sigourney Weaver. Before this happens, our group of oddballs builds a pretty successful business centered around catching and removing ghosts — which, early in the movie, prompts this classic line from Venkman, "We came. We saw. We kicked its ass." They become local celebrities, driving around in their retro-fitted 1959 Cadillac ambulance/hearse with an ECTO-1 license plate, flashing lights and Ghostbusters logo on the side.

However, Spengler becomes concerned about their storage area for the captured spirits and its ability to hold all of them as strange things begin to happen in the city. Then things begin to unravel, and they are visited by the EPA with a court order to shut down their power, causing all the once-captured spirits to escape and wreak havoc on the city. Louis, who now refers to himself as the Keymaster, and Dana who calls herself the Gatekeeper, are possessed by Vinz Clortho and Zuul respectively, who are both minions of Gozer the Destructor, who is hellbent on annihilating New York City and then the rest of the world. Got that? Good. Thankfully we have our Ghostbusters to save the planet from Gozer and a 100-foot-tall Stay Puft Marshmallow Man who has also fallen under the spell of our prehistoric demon seed. The Ghostbusters' approach to saving the city isn't exactly designed after the typical '80s action hero playbook, as seen in this exchange when they confront Gozer the Destroyer:

> **Dr. Raymond Stantz:** "Gozer, the Gozerian ... good evening. As a duly designated representative of the city, county and state of New York, I order you to cease any and all supernatural activity and return forthwith to your place of origin or to the nearest convenient parallel dimension."

> **Dr. Peter Venkman:** "That ought to do it. Thanks very much, Ray."

Bad demon-destroying plans aside, what did our paranormal seeking oddballs teach us about today's workplace:

 The best accelerant for business growth is risk.

When Venkman said, "Why worry? Each one of us is carrying an unlicensed nuclear accelerant on his back," our Ghostbusters were about to use their ghost-busting equipment for the first time in a real-life situation. Even worse, as they are heading up in the elevator to the haunted location, Stantz says, "It just occurred to me that we really haven't had a completely successful test of this equipment." If you are an entrepreneur, small business owner, someone who changed careers or if you secured a job at a higher level than you were prepared for, then you've surely felt the magnitude of an untested moment.

> *If you are an entrepreneur, small business owner, someone who changed careers or if you secured a job at a higher level than you were prepared for, then you've surely felt the magnitude of an untested moment.*

You see, our original three protagonists had just lost their very comfortable jobs at Columbia University and were unexpectedly on the street without a plan. They pretty quickly decide to start a business and promptly purchase an old firehouse through a third mortgage on the house that was left to Stantz by his parents. As Egon and Stantz begin to panic about the interest rates on the loan, Venkman in classic entrepreneur-style says:

"Will you guys relax? We are on the threshold of establishing the indispensable defense science of the next decade — professional paranormal investigations and eliminations. The franchise rights alone will make us rich beyond our wildest dreams."

They quickly create a TV spot that promises a "courteous and efficient staff that is on call 24 hours a day to serve all of your supernatural elimination needs," buy a dilapidated hearse/ambulance complete with sirens as their company vehicle and hang a handwritten sign with the word "Ghostbusters" from the front of their newly acquired building.

Sound familiar? Well, not the paranormal investigations and eliminations part but the whole idea of going for it and jumping in headfirst. Our guys had a service of sorts but little idea of business objectives and principles like understanding your target market, how they were going to pay the bills, and whether there was even a demand for their supply. But they believed and because they believed they took the financial, reputational and physical risks to make a new reality for themselves. **They clearly understood that the best accelerant for business growth is risk.**

There's an old adage about accepting the job or project and then figuring out how to do it, which I don't think included nuclear accelerators strapped to your back, but it makes the point, nonetheless. Today, technology and access to data and analytics has, in some cases, helped with the leap of faith that so many take with a new business or career, but the risks are still the same as before ... or in the words of the Talking Heads from their 1980 hit "Once in a Lifetime," "Same as it ever was, same as it ever was, same as it ever was ..." You get the point, I'm sure.

> ***Today, technology and access to data***
> ***and analytics has, in some cases, helped***
> ***with the leap of faith that so many take***
> ***with a new business or career, but the***
> ***risks are still the same as before.***

I suppose an argument could be made that technology has actually made the risks even greater. Things move at a much faster pace, making speed to market more crucial than ever since competition is also created at an exponentially quicker rate. Just like our Ghostbusters, we sometimes need to get our product or service out before it is fully tested because being first to market has shown to be a distinct difference-maker in terms of success and longevity. Like anything, there are exceptions like Betamax, Netscape, TiVo, Napster and more recently, MySpace, which all prove that being first to market also comes with substantial risk. But it is that risk that should provide the accelerator for growth. Knowing that others will follow should make you want to take the risk to invest more to make your company better; it should make you want to take the risk to believe enough in your offering to put it out in the market before it is absolutely perfect; and it should make you want to take the risk that you might end up with severe nuclear burns.

You absolutely, 100%, cannot grow without risk — not your business and certainly not yourself. I should know. As you read this second book in my series, I have left the comfy confines of the corporate world for the bumpy traipses of being a full-time author and speaker. That risk accelerant? I'm covered in it, but it was the only way for me to create any type of potential for growth. I had to go all-in on this dream, and that meant giving up the security that came with a steady paycheck, 401(k), paid vacation and heavily subsidized benefits. The growth accelerator that is risk applies to career changes as well, and when you see a third book from me, you'll know that "the juice was worth the squeeze."

You absolutely, 100%, cannot grow without risk — not your business and certainly not yourself.

There's a great scene in the movie *Jaws* — I know, I know, it's a 1976 film — but it works here, so bear with me. When the sheriff, the scientist and the shark hunter go out on the water to track down Jaws, the only knowledge they have is that the shark is eating people and it is large. You could say they were taking a risk or two. When they were squarely out on the open water and chumming to attract the shark, it reveals itself, and it is much, much larger than any of them had imagined. This prompts Sheriff Brody to say, "We're gonna need a bigger boat." While this line has been used in modern-day to describe something that is perceived as challenging or even insurmountable, it is exactly the risk that you need to take to accelerate your growth. The longer you take to find the perfect boat, the less likely it is that you will see the shark — which will ultimately allow you to better prepare for the next hunt.

As two of our busters of ghosts said in this classic exchange:

Spengler: "There's definitely a very slim chance we'll survive."

Venkman: "I love this plan! I'm excited to be a part of it! Let's do it!"

Ready. Go. Risk.

Being fired can sometimes be your biggest promotion.

As we mentioned before, it is very early in the movie when our three busters of ghosts are unceremoniously removed from their cushy jobs at Columbia University. Stantz, like most people when they lose their job, is a slight bit concerned about his future and says:

"Personally, I liked the university. They gave us money and facilities. We didn't have to produce anything! You've never been out of college! You don't know what it's like out there! I've worked in the private sector. They expect results."

If you've ever lost your job, particularly when you didn't know it was coming, it feels surreal. I know firsthand. I was let go a few years back when a new CEO came in and removed most of the existing management team. One day, you feel like you are a major contributor to the success of the business, and the next day, you find out that they can go on without you just fine. To view this through an '80s lens — one day you are like the Katrina and The Waves 1985 hit "Walking on Sunshine" and the next day you walk in, and they do their best impersonation of the 1982 hit "Goodbye to You" by Scandal. It's not a great feeling.

But as you saw at the beginning of this chapter, you are far from alone, and some of our best, brightest and most creative leaders and innovators throughout history have been fired from a job. They were better for it, and so are we. The list is long, and we likely wouldn't have The Wonderful World of Disney (Walt Disney), *Harry Potter* (J.K. Rowling), Home Depot (Bernie

Marcus and Arthur Blank) and one global entertainment mogul (Oprah Winfrey) without a handful of pink slips that were likely difficult for management to explain years later.

 FUN FACT: Growing up in Baltimore, I was lucky enough to have John Saunders — the great ESPN broadcaster who passed away in 2016 — as my local sports anchor from 1982 to 1986. From 1976 to 1983, a young Oprah Winfrey was the co-anchor of a local show called *People Are Talking,* and the host of Baltimore's *Dialing for Dollars.* I'd say that is a pretty good news desk.

As strange as it may sound, being fired can sometimes be your biggest promotion. Once you've gotten over the shock and awe, it presents you with a pretty incredible opportunity to figure out who you really want to be. So many of us hurry up to get busy that we end up part of "the mass of men lead[ing] lives of quiet desperation" as Henry David Thoreau so eloquently stated well before the 1980s. Fast forward to the 20th century for a similar sentiment from our buster of ghosts, Venkman, who said, "I don't have to take this abuse from you. I've got hundreds of people dying to abuse me."

It's understandable to feel confused and anxious when we get the proverbial pink slip. Most of us will go through something similar to the Kübler-Ross model's five stages of grief — denial, anger, bargaining, depression, and acceptance. Unfortunately, a lot of people get stuck at one of the stages along the way, but once you realize there is nothing you can do to change it, you get to that last one — acceptance — and this is where the magic happens. This is when you realize that the really great companies and leaders would much rather hire someone who has boldly faced down a challenge rather than someone who has been untested. This is when you realize that your side passion/hustle that occupies the majority of your daydreaming and free time has just recaptured 40-60 hours that are now available and that you can now actually take a run at making it happen. This is when you realize the path that you were on was only one of many that are available to you. This is when you realize that your career and your self-worth should never be determined by one company or manager. This is when you realize that maybe you've been going at this all wrong and have felt the same way as Venkman when he said, "Let me tell you something about myself. I come home from work to my place, and all I have is my work. There's nothing else in my life."

> *This is when you realize that your career*
> *and your self-worth should never be*
> *determined by one company or manager.*

Being fired gives us a chance to reset and rediscover who we are. Take advantage of this moment — embrace it. It's easy to look at it as a negative and feel sorry for yourself in a "Do You Really Want to Hurt Me," Culture Club kind of way, or worse, it's easy to think about how you can get your company to like you again in a Simple Minds, "Don't You Forget About Me" kind of way when they sang, "As you walk on by, will you call my name?" Rather than wallowing for too long in sorrow or self-pity, take a Ghostbusters approach to your situation and attack this temporary obstacle, Peter Venkman-style when he said, "We came. We saw. We kicked its ass!"

Oh, and one more thing we learned from our busters of ghosts. In the workplace and in life, never shy away from **learning on the fly**. As Winston, our fourth Ghostbuster said to Stantz, "When someone asks if you are a God, you say YES!"

CHAPTER 10

THE KARATE KID

"Don't forget to breathe. Very important."

Mr. Miyagi, *The Karate Kid*

Mentors and the practice of mentoring have likely been in practice ever since the first communication between two early humans. Fast forward to 1984 and perhaps the greatest example of mentoring in Hollywood history with Mr. Miyagi and Daniel-san known as *The Karate Kid*. But as you might have seen from past chapters in this book and the previous one, I often eschew the most obvious lessons so we can dig a little deeper into each movie and try to find the unexpected lessons for the workplace.

When Mr. Miyagi said, "Don't forget to breathe. Very important," he was training Daniel in karate basics by washing a car with a disciplined format during the famous wax-on, wax-off scene. The idea was to teach him the patience, consistency, form and mental relaxation needed to be successful at a martial art.

When things become overwhelming at work, we often forget about the importance of staying mentally balanced. Thinking about it now, you can probably feel your teeth beginning to grind a little, your body tightening up and your brain taking you through a million different scenarios (from quitting to dropping a string of f-bombs at the invisible person inside your computer). This is when you have to heed the words of Mr. Miyagi and breathe, because **stress is like dehydration. By the time you realize you have it, it's too late.**

I don't think they could sell a lot of tickets to a movie about a caped crusader whose superpower is efficiency, but it could do well in the corporate training world. When Mr. Miyagi said, "Daniel-san, secret to punch, make the power of the whole body fit inside one inch, here," he was teaching him how to best harness his power and control his energy output during a confrontation.

FUN FACT: I worked for a Japanese company and became fascinated with the culture and their traditions. The "san" on Daniel-san is one of many honor titles in Japanese. It is very common, gender-neutral and can be used to address your equals. While the standard in Japanese culture is to use the last name along with "san," many Japanese will call non-Japanese by their first name with "san" as it tends to be

easier to remember, and most business cultures use the first name.

In the corporate sense, Mr. Miyagi was teaching him about how to best manage the task or project at hand — attack it wisely and be efficient. How many times in the workplace have you heard someone, usually a leader, say, "We need to find ways to be more efficient?" If efficiency was commonplace, then the lack of it wouldn't be a point of discussion at so many levels and within so many companies, which is why **efficiency is absolutely a superpower**. Unlike most superpowers, it should be abused often and used without discretion. And if you see someone with it, treat them as Carol Anne was told to treat the light in *Poltergeist* and "Run to the light. Run as fast as you can" and find a way to get them on your team.

> *In the corporate sense, Mr. Miyagi was teaching him about how to best manage the task or project at hand — attack it wisely and be efficient.*

But before we really expand on our lessons from Daniel-san and Mr. Miyagi, let's hop in our phone booth with Bill and Ted and once again travel back to 1984. Not in an Orwellian-sense. We are way too goofy for that.

It was late June of 1984, and after watching *Ghostbusters* for the third time, my friends and I purchased one more $2.00 ticket at the Village Movie Theatre in Reisterstown, MD, to watch another '80s movie underdog, Daniel LaRusso, fend off his bullies. In between showings, we battled it out at

Pacman, Galaga, Paperboy and Punchout in the makeshift arcade adjacent to the popcorn stand. I still use the classic Punchout verbiage, "Body blow. Body blow. Knock him out" on a daily basis.

This would also be the summer that I gathered several of my friends in the living room of my house to show off our new camcorder and suggest that we make our own adventure movie. As with almost every ridiculous idea teenage boys dream up, it was met with a resounding, "Let's do this thing!" And so the story of *California Bones* was brought to life for the masses to enjoy. The masses, in truth, were our family members, both human and animal as well as a few neighborhood kids who accidentally ended up in a shot and thought that this was going to be their big break. Once they actually saw the movie, even their straight-to-video dreams were completely shattered. Yes, this was one really bad movie, but we had so much fun making it and proudly ruined a few carpets in my house with a concoction of BBQ sauce, ketchup and red food coloring in an attempt to create fake blood. KISS, Ozzy and Alice Cooper would have been proud. We also had a fairly severe smoke bomb incident, but only one person was injured, and thankfully, he had an insignificant part in the film. I'm kidding. Not really though and it was pretty funny. Everyone was fine except for a bit of smoke inhalation.

While we were making the next great homemade movie that only parents could love, the music was continuing to diversify in an awesome way. Julio Iglesias and Willie Nelson teamed up for "To All the Girls I've Loved Before," and just a few spots ahead of them was Van Halen with "I'll Wait." And if the difference between those greats wasn't diverse enough for you, how about we throw in some dance/R&B with Shalamar's "Dancing in the Sheets" rounding out the Top 40 and The Cars holding steady in the Top 20 with "Magic." That song really brings back memories for me from that time. I can almost smell the different flavored popcorn scents emanating from Fishers Popcorn and the unique aroma of Thrashers French Fries (no ketchup allowed, as putting it on their fries was considered utter blasphemy) coming from the Ocean City, Maryland boardwalk in the summer of 1984.

Television was already going reality with *Star Search* giving a platform to amateurs everywhere in an attempt to see their name in Hollywood lights.

FUN FACT: *Star Search* **delivered on its promise throughout the years, providing a stage for unknowns such as Beyonce, Justin Timberlake, Britney Spears, Sinbad, Martin Lawrence, LeAnn Rimes and Alanis Morissette.**

Soap operas were in the prime even without Dr. Drake Ramoray (Joey's famous role from *Friends*), and more were on the way, including the premiere of *Santa Barbara,* which lasted nine years. A run like that is great for a sitcom but considering the most popular soap operas had a lifespan of 30-50 years, you could say that they were the *USFL* (the failed professional football league that tried to compete with the NFL and made it all of three years from 1983 to 1985) of soap opera land. And

the original Impractical Joker, Allen Funt, was in his 36th year
of making people smile by pulling hidden camera pranks
on unsuspecting citizens and celebrities alike with *Candid
Camera.* One of my favorites that I wish someone would
actually remake was in its second year of taking us "down in
Fraggle Rock."

In the past chapters of this book, we've established that the
mid-'80s were an insanely good time at the box office — I mean
it's why I can write these books — and the early summer of
1984 lived up to that reputation. One of the most underrated
comedies of the '80s, *Police Academy*, was finishing up its run
at the box office after 14 weeks of hilarity from Sgt. Tackleberry
and crew while the Roxy battle from *Beat Street* was making me
believe that I could spin across the floor on my back and my
head while maintaining enough balance to throw my hands out
in jest at the rival dance crew. Robert Redford was playing Roy
Hobbs to perfection in *The Natural*, which was also directed
by Barry Levinson from my hometown of Baltimore. He and
John Waters provided quite a bit of Hollywood magic with our
shared hometown as the backdrop in '80s movies like *Diner*
and *Hairspray.*

Opening the week of June 22nd at #5 at the box office was *The
Karate Kid,* starring Ralph Macchio, Pat Morita, Elisabeth Shue
and William Zabka and directed by John G. Avildsen (who
also just happened to direct another little fight film called
Rocky). The Karate Kid tells a story as old as time itself. A kid
(Ralph Macchio) and his mother move to a new town across
the country, where he has trouble fitting into the culture and
his new school. He's picked on and bullied for the crimes of
being new in town and for his accent (he's from Jersey and

now lives in Cali) and then unbeknownst to him he hits on the ex-girlfriend (Elisabeth Shue) of Johnny Lawrence (William Zabka), the leader of the kids trained at the brutal and unforgiving Cobra Kai karate dojo.

FUN FACT: As I have mentioned before, I am not a fan of '80s reboots, but *The Karate Kid* nailed it by opting for a sequel instead and using the original cast to tell the story of Johnny and Daniel 35 years after their fight at the All Valley Karate Championship. As of this writing, it is in season two on YouTube Red, and I'm convinced that its success is the reason that the sequels of *Coming to America* and *Bill and Ted's Excellent Adventure* (forthcoming as of the time of my book's release) are using the original cast in an updated environment.

Daniel eventually ends up in a fight with the Cobra Kai crew, and it is during his second beatdown where he meets Mr. Miyagi (Pat Morita). As he is on the verge of passing out, Mr. Miyagi jumps in and "handles" the gang from the Cobra Kai dojo all by himself, thus saving Daniel from a substantially long stint in a hospital bed.

Mr. Miyagi ultimately agrees to train Daniel-san in the art of karate but not until an exchange that makes it clear where he stands on the true reason for training to fight:

Daniel: "So, karate's fighting. You train to fight."

Miyagi: "That's what you think?"

Daniel: "No."

Miyagi: "Then, why train?"

Daniel: (Pondering) "So I won't have to fight."

Miyagi: "Miyagi have hope for you."

In sharp contrast to Miyagi's approach to the martial arts, Master Kreese at Cobra Kai dojo has an entirely different approach, starting with their motto of "Strike First. Strike Hard. No Mercy." Miyagi takes Daniel to the dojo to see if he can convince Kreese to have his kids leave Daniel alone. When they enter, Kreese is telling the class, "We do not train to be merciful here. Mercy is for the weak. Here, in the streets, in competition, if a man confronts you, he is the enemy. An enemy deserves no mercy."

As you might have guessed, Miyagi fails to convince Kreese to have his class leave Daniel alone, but as he is leaving, he sees a poster for the All Valley Karate Championship. He then asks for a truce if he enters Daniel in the tournament, to which the dojo master agrees. For those of you who haven't seen the movie, I won't spoil it, but I will tell you that there is one spectacular crane kick that hits its mark while the Joe Esposito song "You're the Best Around" is playing in the background. Yeah, it's pretty much a modern-day *Gladiator* movie moment.

So, what did our karate master and his protégé teach us about today's workplace:

Stress is like dehydration. By the time you realize you have it, it's too late.

Ah, the great Mr. Miyagi and his Zen approach to all things life and living through his delicate work on his banzai tree and his philosophically crafted sayings like "Don't forget to breathe. Very important." I remind myself to do this at least 17,000 to 30,000 times a day, which is the average breaths a person takes in a day, and because I'm not that smart, it's imperative that I have a constant reminder. But seriously, think about that for a minute, and during that minute you will breathe roughly 12-20 times without giving it a second thought. Pretty remarkable, actually.

Now, let's do a little test. Take a deep breath and think about the work deliverables you have today, tomorrow, next week or next month. Do you think you will breathe 12-20 times in the next minute or will you unconsciously hold your breath and grind your teeth just a little bit? If you experience any kind of stress at your job, then I'm betting on the latter. Whether it's a few long, deep sustained breaths when you receive an email with a passive-aggressive tone or it's the hold-your-breath-for-fear-of-stringing-multiple-f-bombs-together in a voice loud enough for those around you to hear when you've just been selected as the "hurry up and get this unreasonable task done in an unreasonable timeframe" person, we will all forget to breathe at some point during our workday. Now, *I* can breathe after that super-duper run-on sentence, but I think it made the point (or I hope it did).

**Take a deep breath and think about the work
deliverables you have today, tomorrow,
next week or next month. Do you think you
will breathe 12-20 times in the next minute
or will you unconsciously hold your breath
and grind your teeth just a little bit?**

When Mr. Miyagi is training him in the basics of self-defense,
Daniel becomes frustrated at the pace and the types of exer-
cises he is being asked to do, such as wash Mr. Miyagi's car:
"First, wash all car. Then wax ... Wax on, right hand. Wax
off, left hand. Wax on. Wax off. Breathe in through nose, out
the mouth. Wax on. Wax off. Don't forget to breathe. Very
important." But because Daniel is young and impatient, he
really misses the whole point of the "wax on wax off" exercise.
Rather than the exercise in futility that he thinks it is, Mr. Miyagi
is actually teaching him the value of repetition in the training
of your muscle and mental memory. When confronted in the
future, Daniel will now react quicker and without thinking.
Now, as I mentioned at the beginning of the chapter, the piece
of breathing advice was intended to teach Daniel patience,
consistency, form and mental relaxation. Beyond the memory
training, the car washing was also likely a little lesson in hier-
archy and respect for your elders, which I am beginning to
appreciate as I approach the big *Hawaii Five-0.*

So back to the breathing and what it means for the workplace.
In '80s heavy metal terms, the job stress we feel typically
doesn't hit us fast like the first 30 seconds of Motley Crue's 1989
hit "Kickstart My Heart," but rather like the slow build of the
first 45 seconds of AC/DC's 1980 classic "Hells Bells," climaxing
with the crescendo of an Angus Young guitar solo. Why is that

we allow certain people or tasks at work to affect us in such an unhealthy way? I'm not a psychologist, although I did take an abnormal psych class in college and a class in the psychology of protest music (best class ever), so I can take a run at this. My guess is that it's because we care. We care about doing a good job, and most of us are passionate about what we do. Of course, if there are times when you forget to breathe, you are likely not the passive-aggressive person in the work relationship.

Why is that we allow certain people or tasks at work to affect us in such an unhealthy way?

More and more, we are being asked to keep our human emotions in check and stay just a 1986 Don Johnson *Heartbeat* above flatline. It's understandable that you would make sure you create a work environment that is free of public outbursts full of language that would make even 1980s Eddie Murphy blush just a bit. We certainly don't want to have, as Spicoli put it, a "bogus England place" for an office or business. But there is a reason that things like Rage Rooms — where people pay to break stuff in a variety of ways — are becoming well, all the rage. As our stress builds up and we forget to breathe, there is ultimately going to be a need for an output of sorts. In reality, though, it really shouldn't get to this point.

I remember vividly the only time I had a true case of dehydration and, looking back, the build-up to that point was pretty obvious. I spent four hours playing golf in the very hot South Florida sun; I eschewed drinking water during golf for dipping Skoal chewing tobacco, which does the complete opposite of hydrating the body; went to the gym for a workout and still avoided water; hit the sauna at 190 degrees for 15 minutes supported by a half-glass of water; took a hot shower; went to a sushi bar and ate a lot while drinking large amounts of sake, preferring for some reason to ingest alcohol instead of the water my body so desperately needed.

By the time dehydration had set in, it was too late. I began to feel dizzy and lightheaded; my head and neck broke out in a cold sweat; my legs got very weak; I became nauseated; my vision got blurry, and I started to blackout. It was only when a friend, who owns the restaurant, noticed how *Pale Rider* my face had become that I was saved by Gatorade, water and a cool wet towel on the back of my neck. It took a good three to four days to fully recover, and it taught me a very valuable lesson about hydrating.

All of this is to say that the workplace stress signs are there as well both mentally and physically, but we rarely heed the warnings ... thinking that if we just plow through, it will alleviate itself. But stress really is like dehydration, and by the time you realize you have it, it's too late. As a place to start, when we feel stress at work, we would all be very wise to embrace the words of the great Mr. Miyagi when he said, "Don't forget to breathe. Very important."

Efficiency is absolutely a superpower.

Efficiency isn't exactly a superpower that would get you into the Justice League, The Avengers or even a spot on the much-sought-after Laff-A-Lympics that included 45 of the great Hanna-Barbera characters competing against each other in Olympic sports. No, efficiency just goes about its business and keeps evil villains at bay like Putrid Procrastinator Punk, Dastardly Deadline Disrupter and The Warlock of Waste.

As I mentioned at the beginning of the chapter, when Mr. Miyagi said, "Daniel-san, secret to punch, make the power of the whole body fit inside one inch, here," he was teaching him efficiency in terms of physical confrontation and the defense of oneself. He recognized that in the situations Daniel had faced so far, he was outnumbered and would need to be efficient to be successful and win his battles. On a side note, I was lucky enough to spend a small piece of my career around the UFC (Ultimate Fighting Championship) sponsoring fighters, and I learned a lot from them about discipline, respecting your competition, determination and the absolute importance of efficiency. If you really want to get a taste of how important efficiency is, try punching and kicking the air while moving left to right, forward and back for 60 seconds. Remember, this is with no one to avoid and no one hitting you back. How did you do? Did you really make it 60 seconds? It's tougher than it sounds. Efficiency is absolutely a superpower.

In terms of the workplace, the word efficiency is thrown around quite a bit, but usually in conversations about the lack of it rather than the highlighting of team members who display it. Even with all of the amazing technology we have at our fingertips to help us do our jobs, many companies and teams struggle with efficiency. Part of this may be attributable to the fact that it is both an art and science, which are two very different skillsets. In '80s terms, this is like finding your company's Robin Williams who was able to move back and forth from the comedic *Mork and Mindy* to the dramatic *Dead Poets Society* and somewhere in-between with *Good Morning Vietnam*.

In terms of the workplace, the word efficiency
is thrown around quite a bit, but usually in
conversations about the lack of it rather than
the highlighting of team members who display it.

During my career, I've hired a lot of people, and there are three traits that I look for particularly in entry-level positions: (1) attention to detail, (2) a desire to learn new skills/tools and (3) the ability to focus for longer than the time it takes to read a 280-character tweet. The reason why I look for those traits is that each has a role in creating the whole of efficiency. These also happen to be the three traits that Mr. Miyagi wanted to instill in Daniel through his lessons like washing his car ("Wax on, wax off"), training on the front of the boat ("Breathe in, breathe out and no scare fish") and his choice to use chopsticks over a fly swatter even though he hadn't caught one quite yet. But that's not why I look for these traits. Okay, maybe not the main reason.

Let's break them down:

1. **Paying attention to detail** alleviates most of the unnecessary mistakes or oversights that create additional rounds of review, which will prolong a project and increase the potential for missed deadlines. It can also help to uncover new ideas because the deeper we dig, the more discoveries we make about possible better ways forward for that current initiative. Oh, and I'm terrible at it, so I need team members who can pick me up here. Good leaders know their weaknesses, aren't afraid to admit them and then hire people who have the same trait as a strength. I have lots of

weaknesses, so I need a big team. Being detail-oriented will definitely make you more efficient.

2. **Wanting, better yet, being excited to learn a new skill/ tool** is an excellent way to give your career trajectory a *Knight Rider* KITT-style boost. It's also a huge asset to any team, as the more gaps someone can fill, the quicker the team can get a job done. Team members will be out of the office for a variety of reasons, and if you have someone who can step in and fill a role or skill while someone is out, you minimize the time lost on the project. In baseball and softball, a player who can play multiple positions both in the infield and the outfield is called a utility player. Every team loves having one because they allow the manager to fill gaps that will ultimately arise throughout the season due to injuries, illness, trades, extra-inning ballgames and other team members not delivering as expected. But they are very hard to find, and not every team has one. Being a utility player helps the team to be more efficient.

3. **Being able to focus — really focus —** in this day and age is a superpower in itself. The word "focus" reminds me of cameras so let's put it this way. Back in the day of Polaroid cameras, we really had to focus on getting the right shot and, individually, we had to make sure that we had our look absolutely perfect because once the shot was taken, the picture was coming out for all to see. The Polaroid film was expensive, and you didn't want to waste it. Fast forward to today and, well, you just keep taking the picture over and over again until it is exactly the way everyone wants it. No need to focus on getting it right the first time. In the workplace, the ability to really focus on the task at

hand makes it much easier to see it all the way through at a productive pace that allows the time for colleagues to have a reasonable window to get their part done as well. If your focus can minimize the need for others to have to do "fire drills," then you will be a superhero. Being able to focus helps everyone be more efficient.

I'm not sure which comic book universe or team a superhero whose power is efficiency would actually fit — maybe *Schoolhouse Rock.* I mean they found a way to make a "bill on Capitol Hill" super cool. Or maybe the team from *Guardians of the Galaxy* (I know, I know, not an '80s movie, but so many '80s references and Easter eggs) because they were totally okay with having a talking raccoon and a tree that could only say "I am Groot" as team members. Talk about a lesson in inclusion for the workplace!

All I know is that efficiency is definitely a superpower, and if you are lucky enough to have it, please channel your inner Mr. Miyagi and share it with the next generation. It should be passed down, like our love for '80s movies.

In closing, here's one more nugget from Mr. Miyagi that I think is the perfect end to this chapter and to Book #2 in the "What '80s Pop Culture Teaches Us About Today's Workplace" Series:

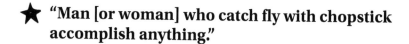 **"Man [or woman] who catch fly with chopstick accomplish anything."**

I hope that reading this book has encouraged you to try new things, manage and communicate differently, bring your best self to work and, ultimately, ACCOMPLISH ANYTHING. Now get out there and go create you!

REFERENCES

Throughout this book, the author has mentioned statistics or other information cited in references that appear in on-page footnotes. The 10 featured movies that inspired the book's corresponding 10 chapters are noted below.

1. *The Outsiders.* Dir. Francis Ford Coppola. Perf. C. Thomas Howell, Matt Dillon, Ralph Macchio, Patrick Swayze, Rob Lowe, Emilio Estevez, Tom Cruise, Diane Lane. Warner Bros, 1983.

2. *The Princess Bride.* Dir. Rob Reiner. Perf. Cary Elwes, Mandy Patinkin, Robin Wright, Chris Sarandon. Twentieth Century Fox, 1987.

3. *CaddyShack.* Dir. Harold Ramis. Perf. Chevy Chase, Bill Murray, Rodney Dangerfield, Ted Knight, Michael O'Keefe. Orion Pictures, Warner Bros, 1980.

4. *Fast Times at Ridgemont High.* Dir. Amy Heckerling. Perf. Sean Penn, Jennifer Jason Leigh, Judge Reinhold, Phoebe Cates, Robert Romanus, Brian Backer, Ray Walston, Forest Whitaker. Universal Pictures, 1982.

5. *The Lost Boys.* Dir. Joel Schumacher. Perf. Jason Patric, Corey Haim, Corey Feldman, Dianne Wiest, Keifer Sutherland, Jami Gertz, Jamison Newlander. Dist. Warner Bros., 1987.

6. *Coming to America.* Dir. John Landis. Perf. Eddie Murphy, Arsenio Hall, James Earl Jones, Shari Headley, John Amos, Eriq La Salle. Dist. Paramount Pictures, 1988.

7. *Better Off Dead.* Dir. Savage Steve Holland. Perf. John Cusack, Diane Franklin, Curtis Armstrong, Amanda Wyss, David Ogden Stiers, Dan Schneider, Kim Darby. Dist. Warner Bros, 1985.

8. *Weird Science.* Dir. John Hughes. Perf. Anthony Micheal Hall, Ilan Mitchell-Smith, Kelly LeBrock, Bill Paxton, Robert Downey Jr. Dist. Universal Pictures, 1985.

9. *GhostBusters.* Dir. Ivan Reitman. Perf. Bill Murray, Dan Akyrod, Sigourney Weaver, Harold Ramis, Ernie Hudson, Annie Potts, Rick Moranis. Dist. Columbia Pictures, 1984.

10. *Karate Kid.* Dir. John G. Avildsen. Perf. Ralph Macchio, Pat Morita, Elisabeth Shue, William Zabka, Martin Kove. Dist. Columbia Pictures, 1984.

ACKNOWLEDGMENTS

Writing a book is such an isolating process and it can be really difficult for someone who considers themselves a bit of an extrovert. But what's really interesting about the process, is although it is a solitary exercise it cannot be done without an incredible team of people that provide support in a multitude of ways. My publisher, Kate Colbert, told me to think of this section of the book — the Acknowledgments — as "my Academy Award Speech." Based on the amount of people I would like to thank, I'm pretty sure the red light would come on, the music would come up and a cane would appear from the side curtain ... yanking me right off the stage. So, here we go:

First, I want to thank everyone who made the investment me and purchased my first book. It is incredibly humbling when someone spends their hard-earned dollars (and their limited time) on your creation. If you are reading this, then you've also made an investment in my 2nd book and, for that, I am also very thankful.

To my family — I am so lucky to have the support of this incredible group of people who have believed in me from the very beginning. Thank you to my **Mom and Dad** for raising me right

(I think) and always supporting my endeavors. Whether it was a move to Florida right after college with $200 bucks in my pocket or quitting the corporate world to pursue this dream, you've always believed in me. Everyone should be so damn lucky. To my sister **Ashleigh,** who inspires me daily and whose courage to pursue her dream encouraged me to pursue mine. I'm a very lucky and a super proud big bro — I love you more than you will ever know. To my **Stepdad and Stepmom** for their unwavering support throughout the years. I also want to thank my Stepdad for his service to our country. Thanks to my Stepbrother **Todd** (Big T) for being a great brother. The "step" in stepbrother has always been non-existent for us and now you get to tell your dates that you are mentioned in an acknowledgement in a book. Love you all.

To all my friends, who put up with my years of '80s movie quotes and a two-year barrage of social media posts, and many of whom wrote great reviews on Amazon to support me. Your continued support and dedication to my dream is what pushes me every day to make this happen. I would love to list everyone here but that might take a book in itself so just know that I see you and I appreciate everything!

Speaking of friends, when you move to a new place like I did and only know one person, the friends that you make become your family. Thank you to this family for taking me in as your own and for all of your support throughout — **Mike Baran, Shawn Silbor, Arad Usha, Harris King, Brittany Conover, Marisa Gillespie (DeMartino), Cory Gillespie, Erin Silbor (Flowers), Stephanie Usha (Faskow), Dana Rhoden, Brian Colon, Nathalie Colon (Vera), Nick Sosa, Travis Brilliant, Pumi Luangrath, Chris Parker,** and **Julia Rosin.**

Thanks to my lifelong friend **Gabe Nardi** for taking me in when I moved to Orlando and to his wife **Tiffany Nardi (Egan)** for somehow allowing me to be the Godfather to their youngest daughter **Presley**. Their oldest daughter **Brooke** escaped that debacle safe and sound. Thanks to **Kevin Geise** for his friendship from the time we met while working at Planet Hollywood in Orlando. Some of my best years were when we were roommates, along with his crazy Jack Russell, **Moose**. Congrats on meeting an awesome woman for life in **Sheila Cortes** (now **Giese**).

Another family who took me in later in my Florida life — 2010, to be exact — are **Top and Lisa** who own **9 Face Sushi** in Pompano Beach. I walked in on one of their first nights of operation and it became my go-to Friday-night spot for amazing sushi and amazing people. We've adopted each other as family — Thai and American. Top's mom has cooked for me when I was under the weather and both Top and Lisa have insisted on delivering it to me even after hours. They are just great human beings. Thank you, Top, Lisa and the team at 9 Face Sushi for being you!

Thanks to my Fantasy Football league ... wait, why am I thanking you? You've been taking my money for years, but not this year. **Cobra Kai** is going to "sweep" the league!

To my good friend, graphic designer and one of my strongest supporters, **Jim Zielinksi**. When I decided to write my first book, I had no idea how I was going to design and produce it. Jim stepped up without hesitation to design my first book and then taught himself how to do the layout and all aspects of the self-publishing process. No easy task and, without him, there's absolutely no way I would be where I am today. He also created the icon illustrations at the top of each chapter in Book #1 and Book #2 in the series.

Thank you to my friend, manager and speaking agent **Kristin Haggar of the Haggar Agency.** For the better part of a year, she coached me from the shadows on how to position myself as a speaker and provided invaluable advice. She has been an absolute rock for me. One of the best days of this journey for me was when I signed the contract to have her represent me in my new career.

To **Christian Boswell**, President of BFW Advertising, for his friendship and mentorship through the years. And to **Sallie Randolph** for her legal advice and her belief in me from the first time we talked.

To the Silver Tree publishing team — **Kate Colbert,** who took me into her amazing stable of authors and made me feel right at home. Even before I was officially on board, she guided me and provided advice for situations with my first book; **Penny Tate,** my project manager, who kept me on track, on time and on my toes; **Courtney Hudson,** who created an amazing cover design that screams '80s and gives us the ability to create a really awesome series (I should also thank her for her patience with an author who is very particular about his brand), and **Hilary Jastram** and **Kate Colbert,** whose editing prowess makes it look like I know how to write.

Thank you to the early readers who provided me with some incredible endorsements: **Dan Leonard** (President of Margaritaville Hospitality Group), **Karen Jones** (EVP and CMO, Ryder), **Joe Cox** (creator of the Pop-Marketer), **Kyle Autrey and**

Justin DiSandro (Back in Time Podcast), **Michael Sherlock** (Shock Your Potential podcast host and two-time business book author), **Ed Saxon** (Academy Award-winning film producer for *The Silence of the Lambs, Philadelphia, That Thing You Do* and many more), **Kevin Barnett** (producer and writer — *Hall Pass, The Heartbreak Kid, The Do-Over* and many more films you know and love), **Jim Garfield** (sports marketing excecutive and professional adventure athlete) and **Meredith Ayan** (Executive Director of SPCA International).

I'd like to thank **Stephen King** for inspiring me with all his writing but in particular his book *On Writing,* which is an absolute must for any author, aspiring or otherwise.

Thanks to **Adam Sandler** for making me laugh through the years and for providing all of us with movies that provide humor with a heart. He also seems to have an affinity for the '80s as well and his movie *The Wedding Singer* was on constantly in the background to set the '80s nostalgia mood as I wrote this book.

Throughout my career, I have worked with some wonderful people in industries and companies across the spectrum. Too many amazing co-workers and human beings to list. There is one who I would like to thank personally and that is **Janine Dodd.** Janine and I met back in 2004 at DHL (during my first stint there) and we would talk '80s movies constantly. I often mentioned doing something around '80s pop culture and she encouraged me to go for it from the very beginning. Thank you, Janine, for your support from literally day one.

I'd be remiss not to thank all the people who didn't return my phone calls or emails over the past few years as I built out my speaking and author career. You inspired me more than you will ever know and made me grind even harder to be successful. Thank you ... and I'm still available for a chat.

A thank you to **Lisa Reynolds** for being the first person to give me a live event stage for my content.

Thanks to **Lisa Ringlen** of Worldwide Business Research for answering my call and then giving me an opportunity to speak at several of the conferences that her team organizes. Lisa, you gave me a chance and I truly appreciate it.

A big thank you to all of you who had me as a guest on your podcasts and gave me the platform to promote my first book: **Win Charles, David Calvert, Kyle Autry** and **Justin DiSandro, David Brower, Al Betz, Chris Voss, Jason A. Meuschke** and **Scott Murray.** And speaking of media — thank you **Tamara G.** of *Those Two Girls in the Morning* for having me on her "Good Morning Miramar" show.

An awesome (totally awesome!) thank you to everyone involved — both in front of and behind the camera — in making '80s movies, '80s music, '80s television and '80s pop culture in general. It goes without saying that you inspired me and were the building blocks for my formative years. I'm so glad to see so many of you back in the spotlight again!

And, of course, a huge Merci Buckets to the wonderful Diane Franklin who wrote a most excellent foreword for this book. She is as cool as she is talented, and never in the craziest dreams of this '80s kid did I ever imagine that Monique from *Better Off Dead* would contribute to a book that I authored. And I love that she's gone from the big screen to the page, and back again, with her own books, like the brilliantly titled *Diane Franklin: The Excellent Adventures of the Last American, French-Exchange Babe of the '80s.*

Lastly, I want to thank my best friend **Dexter Ashford** for whom this book (and this entire series) is dedicated. I thought we would end up old and gray together somewhere on a front porch in our rocking chairs, laughing about stories from our youth, but it was not meant to be. Dex passed way too soon. Fortunately for all of us, his smile will be imprinted on the world for eternity. Thank you, my friend, for so many incredible memories and thank you for continuing to be there for me. I know I can always turn to you when I need support, encouragement or a smile. If you, the reader, ever need to smile, just look at his in the picture at the beginning of this book. It will make your day.

ABOUT THE AUTHOR

Chris Clews grew up in Reisterstown, MD, and is the quintessential child of the '80s, with a closet full of '80s movie t-shirts and a house full of '80s movie artwork. He is an author and keynote speaker on the intersection of '80s pop culture and today's workplace. A huge supporter of animal rescue, he donates a portion of the proceeds from his books and speaking engagements to the SPCA International.

Chris has more than 20 years of marketing experience, and is a graduate of Elon University. During his marketing career, he built brands, led brands through transition, and spearheaded sports sponsorships with NCAA Basketball, PGA, MLB, International Soccer and the UFC. He lives by the words of his favorite poet laureate, Ferris Bueller: "Life moves pretty fast. If you don't stop to look around once in a while, you could miss it."

Chris now spends his time as a writer and keynote speaker at a variety of conferences and events on the topic of '80s pop culture and the lessons that it can teach us for today's workplace. He is the author of an entire series titled *What '80s Pop Culture Teaches Us About Today's Workplace,* which examines iconic movies and their characters, offering up memorable and impactful lessons for workers of all ages, in all industries and at every level of contribution and leadership. This is Book #2 in that series.

KEEP IN TOUCH!

Chris combines his 20+ years of marketing experience in a variety of industries serving global brands and ad agencies with his unmatched passion for all things '80s to bring a fun, interactive, informative, relatable and unique presentation to your group. He calls it "Laugh and Learn" — both of which the audience will do while also discovering valuable lessons for their business, workplace, careers and ultimately themselves.

Ah the 1980s. A magical time for creativity, invention, individuality and timeless movies that taught us valuable business lessons. Wait? What was that last one? *Business lessons?* No matter where you are in your career, the business lessons from these timeless '80s movies will resonate.

So consider hiring Chris to speak at your company, conference, board meeting or major event. You and your audience will:

- Learn what *The Goonies* teaches us about inclusion.

- Hear what Ferris Bueller teaches us about work-life balance.

- Find out how the four kids in *Stand by Me* taught us that there really are no stupid questions.

- See how Axel Foley from *Beverly Hills Cop* taught us how your best resource is you.

- Find out how *The Outsiders* taught us that it's never too late to "create you."

- See how Inigo Montoya from *The Princess Bride* demonstrated the importance of message consistency

- Experience what *The Breakfast Club* taught us about problem solving.

- Learn what *E.T.* teaches us about social responsibility.

- Hear what Jeff Spicoli from *Fast Times at Ridgemont High* taught us about making your business the greatest and coolest place to work.

- Chris brings these and many more lessons from a wide variety of '80s movies.

🌐 **Learn more about Chris and the *What '80s Pop Culture Teaches Us About Today's Workplace* series on his website:**

ChrisClews.com

✉ **Send an email:**

cclews1@gmail.com

@ **Find, follow and share on social media:**

🐦 Twitter.com/80sPopCulture

📘 Facebook.com/ChrisClews80s
Facebook.com/Chris.Clews.10

💼 LinkedIn.com/in/ChrisClews

📷 Instagram.com/ChrisClews80s

If you really enjoyed the book and want to read more, please keep in touch with Chris. Tell your friends and colleagues, leave a review online, or email Chris directly and tell him you want more rad stories about *What '80s Pop Culture Teaches Us About Today's Workplace.*

DID YOU MISS BOOK #1?

Unexpected Business Lessons from 10 of the Greatest '80s Movies that Defined a Generation

Pick up a copy of Book #1 in the series — *What '80s Pop Culture Teaches Us About Today's Workplace: Unexpected Business Lessons from 10 of the Greatest '80s Movies that Defined a Generation* — today to learn dozens of additional lessons about how to relate, achieve and succeed at work, and to take a trip down memory lane with more of your favorite '80s movies and characters.

Book #1 is available in paperback and Kindle editions at Amazon.com.

"You're still here?
It's over.
Go home ... Go."

Ferris Bueller

Chicka Chickaaaa!

Made in the USA
Columbia, SC
20 November 2021

49252028R00120